STUPIDITY

A MATTER OF OPINION

This is a book about opinions. It is a misguided tour with no real beginning or end, but one which passes some interesting places on the way. Opinions require knowledge and a quest for knowledge is a defining characteristic of civilisation. Yet total knowledge, let alone complete understanding, always escapes us; it is an elusive destination. This collection of opinions is called *A Dictionary of Idiocy* for two reasons. First, it is a snappy title. Second, it revives a neglected phenomenon: what the French call a 'sottisier' and we would call a collection of howlers, or perhaps, platitudes. Besides, idiocy itself needs a re-tread. 'Idiocy' has come to mean a deficient intellect, almost synonymous with stupidity, which the dictionary says is a slowness of mental processes. But originally, an 'idiot' was a private man. This is the form of idiocy we are examining here: the private man with opinions of his own.

The nineteenth-century French novelist Gustave Flaubert made this subject his own more than a hundred years ago. He soon realised the problems of cataloguing opinions. The whole process involves a corrosive relativism that can be intellectually and physically exhausting. 'My deplorable mania for analysis is doing me in', Flaubert said in a letter to his confidante, George Sand. Their relationship was one of literature's great *amitiés amoureuses*. In their correspondence he revealed his almost continual intellectual torment. In December 1874 he said 'I am mortally depressed. When I'm not fretting about my work, I moan about myself'. Later he added, 'I belong to another world'.

Flaubert seems, while defining himself as an artist, almost literally, to be defining himself as an idiot. But that is absurd: Flaubert was a genius of the first water.

He used his ambitious and flawed novel *Bouvard et Pécuchet*, unfinished on his death in 1880, as a vehicle to explore the possibilities and purposes and imponderable dangers of acquiring perfect knowledge. Flaubert's two heroes, in a way symbols of himself, wanted to understand everything and, predictably, became confused. The more we learn, the less we understand. Bouvard and Pécuchet became dismally *perturbé* as they attempted to acquire all the world's knowledge, but found themselves confronted and all but paralysed by their own ignorance. And, indeed, that of the world.

Flaubert resolved his deplorable mania for analysis by becoming interested in opinions. No one is ever very happy about opinions. But what is an opinion? The thesaurus offers: belief, conviction, idea, persuasion, view, feelings, inclination, sentiment, bias, speculation, supposition, estimation, judgement. The dictionary defines them as 'judgements resting on grounds insufficient for complete demonstration'. Which is to say imperfect knowledge. There are perhaps three types of opinion. The first is the educated man's opinion that certain popular beliefs are stupid. The second is the sort that drove Flaubert to near madness, the opinion that certain original thoughts are stupid. Third, there is the conventional 'wisdom' about what is correct.

Imagination, Victor Hugo said, is intelligence with an

A DICTIONARY OF IDIOCY

by

STEPHEN BAYLEY

GIBSON SQUARE

This edition published in 2012 by

Gibson Square Books Ltd
info@gibsonsquare.com
www.gibsonsquare.com

ISBN 9781906142629
eISBN 9781908096784

Printed by CPI Group (UK) Ltd, Croydon, CR0 4YY

A Dictionary of
IDIOCY

by

Stephen Bayley

erection. In a similar way, an opinion is knowledge that has been given a particular direction. Unmediated knowledge is just data, dull and meaningless. Opinions are informed patterns of thought, they are what makes knowledge valuable. And controversial. Opinions need to be based on fact, but the distance between assembling facts and forming opinions can be surprisingly long. Hence the crisis of *Bouvard et Pécuchet*, hence Flaubert's inclusion of his celebrated — but neglected — *Dictionnaire des idées reçues* as an appendix intended to be a supportive prop to the wobbly literary conceit of his novel.

There are a number of exquisite conflicts here. As the product of a private man's thoughts, opinions approach the original meaning of idiocy. The great thing in writing about idiocy is that you cannot be wrong. In dealing with this subject, no critic can upbraid the writer for error, misconception or omission, a thrilling release from conventional restraints. And a fine protection from objections about incompleteness.

Original opinions are as rare now as they were in Flaubert's day. There is a character in a nineteenth-century novel who says 'I never offered an opinion till I was sixty … and then it was one which had been in our family for a century'. Opinions only flourish in periods or cultures without a dominant religion. A medieval monk in his Cluniac abbey or a contemporary mullah in his mosque or, indeed, a fine Victorian gentleman, had little use for original opinions. The collective opinions of religion are inflexible dogma, not interesting expressions of private thought.

The best ones are contrarian, not conformist, although that is, of course, in itself a matter of opinion. It is this irreverent quality that attracted Flaubert, the perpetual adolescent. And it was for the same reason that the Duke of Wellington disapproved of his soldiers cheering because this was very nearly an expression of a personal opinion and, by suggestion, insubordination or even mutiny.

Thus there is a hint of modernist rebellion about the opinion. Opinions may become collective, but they are initiated by individuals. So by the early twentieth century, when rebelliousness had become a touchstone of creativity, opinions were beginning to be valued. In *A Mathematician's Apology* (1940), which has been described as a book of haunting sadness, G.H. Hardy says 'It is never worth a first-class man's time to express a majority opinion. By definition, there are plenty of others to do that.'

Hardy, an Oxbridge mathematician whose interests were diophantine analysis and the zeta function, was a fine example of an opinionated individual. A technical genius, and something of an idiot, his 1908 *Course of Pure Mathematics* changed the way universities taught the subject. A troubled soul who once attempted suicide, Hardy was an extremely private man. So much so that only five photographs of him exist. He could not abide mirrors and in hotels covered them with towels. He took what he called his 'anti God battery' to cricket matches: dressing against the prospect of inundation, he dared God to make it rain. Like Flaubert, Hardy was dismayed by the crassness and ignorance of contemporary life, 'the confident, booming, imperialist, bourgeois English' as he described them.

What Hardy called 'majority opinions' were what Flaubert damned as bourgeois conformism. Inevitably, in formal societies, as in the Duke of Wellington's army, the expression of independent opinions is dangerous. Or at least, disrespectful. Ghosts of this sense cling to our modern use of the word. When someone says 'that's a matter of opinion' it is a contemptuous, not a respectful, remark. Few people feel themselves flattered when told they are 'opinionated', yet to have opinions is one of the great privileges of modern life. There is, as we said above, no such thing as a medieval opinion. There was medieval philosophy, theology and rhetoric, but their content and scope and direction were rigidly defined.

Opinions are in a creative hierarchy that has at its base axioms, or self-evident truths. Next come epigrams, short, witty sayings which are valid in one particular case and have no general relevance. Then there are aphorisms, clever statements which contain a general truth. Aphorisms are usually nowadays of a literary character, although they began with medicine. For Hippocrates sharp observations were a means of recording the progress of knowledge. '*Ars longa, vita brevis* — art is long, life is short' is a Hippocratic aphorism.

The best aphorists have been inspired by man's stupidity. The Duke of La Rochefoucauld illustrated very brightly the laughable hypocrisy and depressing small-mindedness which are familiar traits in stupid humankind. His *Réflexions, ou sentences et maximes morales* (1665) is a masterpiece of cynical, contrarian opinion-forming.

Perhaps because of a readily made association with the very fine Monsieur le Duc, W.H. Auden thought aphorisms were aristocratic since the successful aphorist never felt any compunction to explain or justify his loftily superior position. So La Rochefoucauld said '*C'est un grande habileté que de savoir cacher son habileté* — It's a great talent to be able to hide your talent', and that was that. It was the same with Blaise Pascal, although he was an altogether different character. The element of misanthropy appearing in Pascal (in, for example, his most famous maxim '*Plus je rencontre de gens, plus j'aime mon chien* — the more people I see, the more I love my dog') is common to all treatments of stupidity.

In a richly perverse way, which Flaubert sensed, but found confounding, an awareness of stupidity is a defining characteristic of intelligent life, a survival characteristic. Interestingly, the northern Europeans seem to have something of a monopoly in the subject. A best-seller of the late Middle Ages was Sebastian Brant's *Das Narrenschif.* First published in 1494, this went into French as *Le Nef des fous* and was Englished by Alexander Barclay as *The Shyp of Folys of the World* in 1509. Possibly inspired by Columbus' voyage, Brant used the motif of a crowded boatload of storm-tossed unfortunates to satirise and catalogue the fascinating variety of human folly and weakness. Erasmus, Rabelais, Cervantes, Pope and Sterne also concerned themselves with stupidity. Cervantes' *Don Quixote,* '*el caballero de la triste figura* — the knight of woeful countenance', is the quintessential idiot. A private man, a man of opinions, at odds with the dull conformity of his world.

Great minds think alike and fools, it is said, never differ. That is a collective opinion. But in my opinion it is wrong: great minds are almost always singular. Alexander Pope's 'confederacy of dunces' slipped easily into the language, rather suggesting a general acknowledgement that stupidity is commonplace. Certainly that was what Flaubert believed as he battled against the entrenched stupidity of the middle-classes, with their platitudes and their worthless, dull opinions. His weapons in the battle were knowledge and wit. But acquiring that knowledge drove him to physical breakdown. So we have to wonder was Flaubert's self-destructiveness stupid or not?

Around 1910, when the Louis Conard edition of *Bouvard et Pécuchet* was published, Ambrose Bierce wrote an essay entitled 'Some Disadvantages of Genius'. He complained that geniuses are often not understood, then — perhaps realising this was an idiotic thing to say — promptly went to Mexico and was never seen again. Genius and madness are close, but so are idiocy and high intelligence. Neither seems to be well understood.

What follows is a collection of modern opinions. Such a collection is certainly an idiotic undertaking. Yet it is designed to make one stop being stupid. Or, at least, to disguise it. There's a lot to be said for this version of idiocy. Wittgenstein believed if people never did idiotic things, nothing intelligent would ever happen. In this sense human progress depends on the continuing practice of forming opinions. So progress, or at least a form of it, is assured. Starting here. If you are idiotic, you are civilised. Some may find that a challenging opinion.

ABSTRACTION

This is the determination to paint absolutely nothing, a quest which Rosalind Kraus said the first abstract painters took 'very seriously indeed'. Abstract painting is one of the great artistic innovations of the modern age, but also one of the most nugatory and ruinous.

Its sources are everywhere in the nineteenth century. When Hazlitt criticised a Turner for being 'tinted steam and little else' he had detected the troubling basis of the abstract idea. Equally, the exploration of pictorial structure begun by Paul Cezanne led to the final analysis of a painting as an arrangement of flat colour on a flat canvas. Its rationale can also be found in the imagist poetry of Stephane Mallarmé. '*Peindre non la chose, mais l'effet elle produit*—Don't paint the thing, just the effect it produces'. With the invention of photography it was frequently said that 'from today, painting is dead'.

Abstraction used to be the sharp, cutting edge of art history. Now it is genteel, refined, harmless, rather like serious jazz— with which it has much in common. The big ideas it once represented are now mainstream and its shock value usurped by more daring pranksters.

Something which is abstract, properly speaking, is something that has to be considered in its own right rather than in reference to anything else. To take something in the abstract is to do so out of context. Abstract painting evolved from the debate about the role of figurative art (essentially a form of illustration, a term artists use derisively) after photo-mechanical processes had usurped its ability to provide the world with faithful images of man and nature.

Many pioneer abstract painters (Kandinsky and Mondrian, for instance) were involved in theosophy and other loopy forms of speculative mysticism. When Alexei Jawlensky said '*Ein Kunstwerk ist ein Welt, nicht ein Nachahmung der Natur*—A work of art is a universe, not an imitation of nature' he offered a thrilling freedom from the sterile strictures of academic painting, but also justified indulgent solipsism. Kasimir Malevich was the most unworldy of them all and hilariously explained 'The square is an expression of binary thought [which] distinguishes between impulse and no impulse, between one and nothing'.

Notably, most abstract painters were not WASPs (White Anglo-Saxon Protestants). Their champion was the critic Clement Greenberg, himself a ghetto child. This anti-establishment art had a clear attraction for a polemicist who felt himself an outsider. So much had Kandinsky, Rothko and Kline associated abstract art in the American imagination with eastern Europe that the US media had to invent their own homespun abstract hero. This was Jackson Pollock, from Cody, Wyoming. He was well able to match the mystification of his rivals from beyond the pale. In 1950 he told *The New Yorker* 'Abstract painting is abstract. It confronts you.'

ACADEMICS

The general term to describe teachers and researchers devoted to study for its own sake has a revealing etymology. The first academy, a hermetic group of teachers and students, was founded by Plato in his garden. Ever since, academics have favoured isolated situations above the hurly-burly of the mundane, notably ivory towers (from the French *tour d'ivoire*, a familiar nineteenth-century literary expression). Remote locations are preferred so as to retain an imagined integrity. Another definition of academic is 'not leading to a decision or unpractical'. Therefore, to describe something as 'academic' is to stigmatise it as irrelevant. It is important not to confuse an academic with an intellectual because they are not the same thing. Intellectuals believe in ideas; academics depend on systems to keep them going.

When Tom Dixon entered the senior common room of his

university in Kingsley Amis' landmark novel *Lucky Jim* (1956) his shocked reaction to the squalor and torpor of the environment and its occupants was an echo of the author's own experience as an English lecturer in Swansea in 1955. But academics are not only given to idleness, slobbery and cultivated high-brow boorishness, academics are also famous for their bitching. Two of Britain's leading historians had a famous exchange. The maverick A.J.P. Taylor (who coined the term 'Establishment' in 1953 and lived an anti-Establishment life, at its very core, for thirty or so more years) once expressed the opinion that 'In international affairs there was nothing wrong with Hitler except that he was German'. His rival, the more slippery Hugh Trevor-Roper (who, as Lord Dacre, authenticated the bogus Hitler diaries while in the pay of *The Sunday Times,* who published them), wrote of Taylor's *The Origins of the Second World War* that it would 'do serious harm' to his 'reputation as a serious historian'. Taylor, incensed at Trevor-Roper's misleadingly selective quotation said Trevor-Roper's 'methods ... might all do harm to his reputation as a serious historian, if he had one.'

Although often belligerent and opinionated, academics are also famously reluctant to reach conclusions, citing the principle that 'more research is required' in order to forestall the energetic activity of jumping to conclusions.

Although often intellectually belligerent, academics are frequently reluctant to make up their minds. It is a nice paradox that a tribe so unwilling to take the exercise of jumping to conclusions should be such a rich source of idiotic opinions.

ACCOUNTANTS

Accountants are the most detested of the professions. Retrospection is their trade. The odour of sanctity is their style. They exchange style for caution and practise a timid sort of superiority. Growing slick and suave on bankruptcies and liquidations, they leach money the while from small businessmen. While in the United States business is run by lawyers (with the result that the 1993 contract to supply the White House with a new $25m switchboard ran to 12,000 pages) and in France 'Administration' is taught as a prestige post-graduate subject, in Britain the professional manager is an accountant. One consequence of this is that British industry is run by individuals whose mental furniture is arranged in short-term displays. If you have been trained to construe all human endeavour in terms of annual budgets, cashflows, audits, balances, and annual profits and losses you may not have the necessary speculative intelligence to invest in daring ideas.

This conservatism is enshrined in Britain in the Institute of Chartered Accountants' *Guide to Professional Ethics* which insists on 'integrity' which it defines as actions uncorrupted by self-interest or truth. But, as Picasso—one of the truly turbulent creative geniuses—said, great artists don't borrow, they steal. As for fair-dealing, creative types prefer unfair dealing. There is a demand for 'objectivity', defined as 'the state of mind which has regard to all considerations relevant to the task in hand, but no other' which excludes the possibility of uninhibited free-thinking. On expertise it says '… a member should undertake professional work only where he has the necessary competence required'. This inhibits daring innovation. Risk-taking, tolerance of error, are all necessary to creativity. Picasso said he was always doing what he did not know how to do to find out how to do it. Yet it was the same spirit which brought us the modern city, the modern state, science.

And the bourgeois mentality also gave rise to the professional accountant. Renaissance rationalism demanded order in business practices. So it is depressing to compare the banality of the modern accountant with the richness of his intellectual inheritance. Perhaps the first modern book of accountancy was the *Liber Abaci*, a study of the abacus, of 1202 by the Pisan mathematician, Leonardo Fibonacci. At about the same time in Germany, the very first ledgers were being kept: the increasing complexity of international trade made it necessary methodically to record transactions, while hitherto it had been the habit of merchants merely to stick notes of trades onto their walls.

The great intellectual breakthrough which gave rise to modern accounting was double-entry bookkeeping (*partita doppia* in Italian, *doppelte Buchhandlung* in German) a simple procedural innovation which allowed immediate understanding of assets and liabilities, an essential concept in the development of capitalism, comparable in its way to the discovery of gravitation or the circulation of the blood. The techniques of double-entry bookkeeping had been established by Cotrugli in his *Della Mercatura* (1458) but it was another mathematician, the Franciscan friar, Fra Luca Pacioli, a friend of the painter Piero della Francesca, who refined them. Pacioli, an adept of sacred geometry, dealt with book-keeping in his *Summa di arithmetica, geometria, proportioni e proportionalità* (1494).

While there are more than one hundred thousand accountants in Britain there is no working definition of the profession: anyone can call himself an accountant, although few people would wish to do so.

ADVERTISING

Advertising is one of the great cultural forms which distinguishes the twentieth century. In the sense that advertising helps mould and project and define popular expectations of life it can be compared to art. The child psychiatrist Bruno Bettelheim said, in *Recollections and Reflections* (1990), that advertising is a 'part of the literature to which the child is exposed earliest'. While it may not be the oldest profession, a remark by John Hegarty, one of Britain's leading exponents, that 'I'm just a tart' does offer another less charitable perspective. The well-known art director Lester Bookbinder described the creative director's role in advertising as 'turning crap into mediocrity', perhaps an unconscious reference to the philosopher George Santayana's view that the purpose of advertising was to make 'the worse appear the better'.

Nonetheless, the groundswell of opinion suggests that advertisers do not, on the whole, sell themselves well. In 1887 Henry Ward Beecher wrote in his *Proverbs from a Plymouth Pulpit* that 'The advertisements in a newspaper are more full of knowledge in respect to what is going on in a state or community than the editorial columns are'. Yet to George Orwell, advertising was 'the rattle of the stick in the swill bucket'. Baudelaire said ads were 'nausea'. Paul Valéry believed advertising had 'annihilated the power of the most powerful adjectives'. But the most articulate early attack on advertising came from the Arts and Crafts poet, illustrator and upholsterer, William Morris, whose 1896 polemic against the pernicious spread of billboards across hitherto unspoilt (and poor) countryside was presented as a paradigm of the ruination which industrialised processes did to Nature. Ogden Nash had the same notion, but expressed it more humorously in his poem 'Song of the Open Road' (1929):

> I think that I shall never see
> A billboard lovely as a tree
> Indeed, unless the billboards fall
> I'll never see a tree at all.

The best book about advertising, the one that describes the evolution from primitive claims to the more sophisticated and manipulative imagery we enjoy today, was Rosser Reeves' *Reality in Advertising* (1961). This is the source of the handy notion 'Unique Selling Proposition', used to good effect for the purposes of this book.

AFRICA

When John Lok discovered Africa in 1562 he found a country

with 'A people of beastly living, without a God, lawe, religion ... whose women are common for they contract no matrimonie, neither have respect to chastitie ... whose inhabitants dwell in caves and dennes for these are their houses and the flesh of serpents their meat ... They have no speech, but rather a grinning and chattering.' 'There are', he helpfully added 'people without heads, having their eyes and mouths in their breasts'.

This is not true, although echoes remain. In the thirties, Nazi aesthetes were so alarmed at the disruptive energy of modern art with its direct line to primordial African sources of energy that they organised a huge 'Entartete Kunst' (Degenerate Art) exhibition where the test of depravity was the extent to which painters and sculptors appeared to be African. Equally, the 'Kunstbolschewismus' of modern architecture reviled by the Nazis had a partial source in Africa: the light-shade *chiaroscuro* of sunlit North African vernacular buildings was certainly an influence on Le Corbusier and in his influential book, *Architecture without Architects*, Bernard Rudofsky drew the attention of a generation of architects to the dramatic purity of form of 'primitive' structures.

AMERICAN ENGLISH

'Unselected rollback to idle' is American English for an aircraft engine failure. The greatest medium for intellectual and personal exchange, American English is even more adaptive than British English, itself a mongrel language. American English is also more inconsistent than British English. It can receive new words even more directly.

American English has gone through a series of influences. First was Puritanism. The same taste for piety that made them board the Mayflower in the first place also inspired the Puritans to a severe strictness with language, an influence which lasted well into the nineteenth century and culminated in Noah Webster's expurgated Bible of 1833. Soon there followed a completely different influence, the Industrial Revolution with its new vocabulary and the stimulus of social mobility. Waves of immigration then provided further innovations.

The poet Walt Whitman, not quite, but nearly, a national figure, inspired great breadth in American English literature by broadening the subject matter of his poetry. Then followed Hollywood, radio and television. These new communications media brought with them new influences, new attitudes and soon new words. As language is perhaps the most accurate reflection of a nation's preoccupations, comparisons to British and American English are cruelly revealing of local foibles.

You can make a fascinating cross-cultural comparison by looking at words that have been invented over the past two hundred years. The first list is a sample of British inventions (with the name of the person responsible in brackets) International (Bentham), Intensity (Boyle), Hallucination (Sir Thomas Browne), Diplomacy (Burke), Propriety (Mrs Burney), Bored (Byron), Captain of Industry (Carlyle), Picnic (Chesterfield), Pessimism (Coleridge), Agnostic (Huxley), Literature (Johnson), Gloom (Milton), Gruesome (Scott), Fairy Tale (Tennyson).

Words invented in British English have the function of describing either literary moods or political ideas. The inventions of words in American English on the other hand often have their source in some form of expertise. Wherever, American English has a marked tendency to complexity. Thus, a turkey sandwich is described as 'Roast free range Rhode Island turkey with caramelised Vidalia onions and basil on a toasted baguette.' In Britain, topographic and gastronomic references create a pretentious complication intended to excite favourable anticipations of sophistication. Alternatively,

American English as the language of a culture specially dependent on technology has evolved various sesquipedalian expressions to defuse bad news about machinery which, if more expressive or less wayward, would be alarming. Thus 'Houston, we have a problem' is a nice understatement.

Americans, under the continuing influence of Puritanism, also tend to favour the euphemism more than the British. These take a number of forms fascinatingly revealing of American obsessions. For instance, borrowing from classical languages confers a specious dignity. Thus micturition is American for 'pee' (urine). The same effect can be achieved by a lordly aggrandising and enlarging of terms, thus 'solid human waste' for shit. And then there is the cute tendency for diminution, as when 'hind end' (i.e. bum) becomes 'heinie'.

But it is in the area of technology and technically inspired terms, often related to war, that American English has so richly extended the limitations of the mother tongue. Thus, a retreat becomes 'exfiltration'. 'Climactic disturbances at the air-sea interface' means heavy waves. 'This entry is in the early states of finalisation' which means unfinished. Lately, computer terminology has further enriched the language. Acronyms are also a rich and evocative source of novelty: DGZ means 'desired ground zero', a complicated way of saying 'target'. ROM, meaning 'Read Only Memory', a technical term for a simple-minded electronic component, has acquired a useful metaphorical function as a description of an individual of small intelligence.

ARCHITECTS

He stood naked at the edge of the cliff. The lake far below him. A frozen explosion of granite burst in flight to the sky over motionless water. The water seemed immovable, the stone flowing. The stone had the stillness of one brief moment in battle when thrust meets thrust and the currents are held in a pause more dynamic than motion.

The stone glowed, wet with sunrays.

Prose does not come any more purple than the opening passage of *The Fountainhead*, Ayn Rand's 1947 novel about Howard Roark, a headstrong, visionary architect. When Warner Brothers made the movie two years later, Gary Cooper was cemented in the lead role. Studio publicity shots show him staring with steel beam rigidity at some utopian objective, his cantilevered jaw a symbol of moral resolution. Rand was the founder of the self-help 'philosophy', Objectivism, and it seemed natural for her to cast an architect as a Leader of Society.

Interestingly, the progress of any civilisation can be calibrated by the founding of *the professions*. The chronology betrays status: first came the barristers in the fifteenth century and they are still on top of the pile. Then came physicians in 1518; solicitors in 1739 and surgeons in 1745. Architecture only became a recognised profession in 1834 when the Institute of British Architects was established. This was forty three years after the Royal Veterinary College ... Perhaps naturally for the British, our esteem for specialists who treat ringworm or hardpad is greater than that for the specialists who build cathedrals and universities. In terms of professional pedigree, architects can only lord it over chemists (1841), actuaries (1848) and dentists (1855).

While the other professions grew out of the clergy, buildings were needed before any church was established, thus architecture does have a claim to being the oldest profession. In Freemasonic ritual God is called the chief architect of the Universe, a vocation that is hard to ignore. While no one is ready to forego the advantages of living in buildings, it is astonishing how much opprobrium the architect attracts. No other profession — with the possible exception of accountancy — is so generally despised.

Maybe as self-defence, the architect's response to the gravity of his practical and cultural obligations has always been to assume the posture of Universal Genius. In *The Fountainhead*, Howard Roark tells his principal 'I have nothing further to learn here'. The bravura world-view of the architect finds external expression in carefully nurtured images which the public often finds indigestible. Frank Lloyd Wright, who seems to have been the model for Howard Roark, had a weakness for suede underwear and dramatic headgear, and favoured a blue rinse. Today, the architect is likely to present himself either as a cool technocrat or a suave bohemian.

In either case great careers are made by a magnificent insistence on countenancing the needs of a client. Richard Rogers' Lloyds Building in the City of London — indubitably a work of genius — was designed virtually in defiance of the tastes and requirements of the people who paid for and used the building. Equally, the practical, artistic and financial disaster that was the Millennium may in part be attributed to problems arising from the design of the Dome which, absurdly, pre-dated any plans for what to put in it.

ARISTOCRACY

Aristocracy, if you go back to the Greek, means government by the best of men. The word no longer has this meaning. Britain has an aristocracy in place of an intelligentsia. Its power is based on land tenure. The association of class with property has tended to make the aristocracy mean, almost as a defining characteristic. Like all privileged cliques, they have developed a language of their own. If Lord someone who owns 100,000 acres in Scotland is heard hissing 'DCSC' across the dinner table he is communicating the ungenerous message 'Don't carve second chicken'. Lord Caldecott was said to be able to carve a grouse for twelve. Secondly, despite their affable nature and their disclaimers about privilege, aristocrats are exclusive and use codes of behaviour to maintain that exclusivity. In his marvellous book about snobbery, P.N. Furbank offers the following mind-bender; 'Lord Beauchamp thought it middle class *not* to decant champagne.' These minutiae are full of revelatory detail. The fishknife, an invention of High Victorian middle-class gentility, is reviled by aristocrats. In his autobiography, *Well, I forget the rest* (1991) Quentin Crewe says his mother had never even *seen* a fishknife until her second marriage. The Duchess of Devonshire, Nancy Mitford's sister, explained that it was vulgar to comment on food or art. This systematic and entrenched refusal to embrace the life of the mind is a defining characteristic of the aristocrat. The unreflecting tribal prejudices of the aristocracy do not encourage the athletic life of the mind that leads to the creation of original opinions.

ART

According to E.H. Gombrich, 'There is no such thing as art ... only artists'.

AVANT-GARDE

It is a beguiling paradox that nowadays there are few things more passé than the avant-garde. An expression once used to give cachet to the expeditionary forces of art, the avant-garde belongs to that period when culture was a battlefield. When artists were busy throwing pots of paint in the public's face, creativity could be quantified by capitalising on offence — hence the appropriateness of the nom-de-guerre for the shock troops. When outrage was a measure of freshness, a talent to distress was confused with the ability to enlighten. Nowadays we get our outrage and our distress elsewhere, in newsagents, traffic and on the street.

Yet, redundant and bereft of meaning, we are still living with the afterlife of the avant-garde: the idea that art has leaders and followers imposed a structure on our imaginations which has been difficult to shift. During the nineteenth century, the growth of mass consumption undermined the notion that art was meant to cause delight. Culture was not a consensus, but instead actually represented opposition to the tastes of the booming marketplace. Stripped of their public, artists did not know whether they were meant to be leaders or outsiders, creators or conformists.

The conflict is expressed by the classicist Charles Percier: 'The true perfection of every art consists less in the discovery of unknown things than in the judicious use of those elements already sanctioned by custom and taste.' Contrast this with Baudelaire's opinion that 'The chief task of genius is precisely to invent a stereotype.'

The avant-garde artist aimed to *'épater les bourgeois'*. This was exactly what Albert Jarry did when he shocked the audience at the first performance of his play 'Ubu Roi' with the opening line '... *Merde!*' It is perhaps a measure of the durability of the avant-garde that nowadays this is all that is remembered of Jarry's script.

BATHROOM

The idea of cleanliness being next to Godliness does not have the sanction of history. Indeed, for long periods the Catholic Church was passionately opposed to bathing since it was thought to excite sexual appetites and to cater to an unseemly vanity. In his *Ad Eustochium Virginem* (For the Virgin of Eustoch), St Jerome says *'Dicens munditiam corporis atque vestitus animae esse immunditiam —* The purity of the body and its garments mean impurity of the soul'. Between the Fall of Rome and the early modern period, the habit for bathing was all but forgotten in Europe. Consequently, the rules of the great Burgundian abbey at Cluny called for no more than three towels to cater for the needs of the entire community.

One for the novices, one for the professed and one for the lay brothers. Monks generally took two baths a year. As late as the end of the seventeenth century, Madame de Mazarin, having entered the convent at Vistandines, expressed a modest desire to wash her feet. She was reproved as immodest by the abbess and her request firmly denied.

The progress of the bathroom from being a closet for intimate ablutions, to be dealt with surreptitiously and without ritual or ceremony, to a showpiece—occasionally for entertaining—has consequently been slow. Yet there has never been any doubt that the provision of hygiene has always been a mark of civilisation. In his landmark book about the history of manners, *Moeurs Intimes du Passé* (1909), August Cabanès says formalised bathing is '*un de ces besoins instinctifs commandés par la nature*—one of those instinctive needs ordained by nature'.

For this reason the bathroom has a political character. A bolshevik once remarked that there could not be any revolution in the United States as the citizens were too clean. 'You can't feel revolutionary in a bathroom', he reluctantly conceded. But you can feel a lot of other things, embarrassment being the most familiar and the least fortunate. A unique set of verbal evasions—smallest room, the geography—are evidence of the bathroom's symbolic importance in our lives. The bathroom is the necessity we like best to avoid. In American English, 'bathroom' is a euphemism for lavatory.

This anxiety about bodily functions goes very deep in Western culture. It is not, as one might assume, simply a trait of sexually repressed Anglo-Saxons. Even Greeks vaguely refer to the lavatory as '*to menos* – the place'. The oldest term in English is 'privy', immediately suggestive of seclusion and intimacy, just like (water) closet. Havelock Ellis explained in his monumental *Studies in the Psychology of Sex* (1900) the basis for the bathroom taboo:

Careful study of the nuances of taboo shows that it lessens in proportion to the distance of the part of the body in question from any part of the body possessed by even secondary sexual functions ... It is this anatomical proximity which has imposed a much stricter verbal taboo upon going to the lavatory than, for example, upon cleaning the teeth or cutting the nails, both of them operations which may be referred to, but not performed, in public.

BEARDS

According to Justinus Valerianus Vannetti, *Barbalogia* (1760), Adam was born with a beard, but not—according to the great European pictorial tradition—with pubic hair. Hairiness has been related to strength since the Greeks, although Alexander the Great did insist that his soldiers were clean shaven lest the beard might serve as handles for the enemy (rather as it is sometimes held that muttonchop whiskers—bugger's grips— may facilitate successful male intercourse). Since it is a sign of masculine dignity and strength, man's chief secondary sexual attribute, an assault on the beard is impudent, hence the English expression 'to beard' someone means to tease or contradict. However, in French *'être barbant'* means 'to be boring'—'*La barbe!*' means what-a-bore! Facial hair has almost always attracted opprobrium: our term 'bigot' seems to be derived from the Spanish *bigote* for moustache, thence into Norman as *bigoz* meaning people with hairy faces. In an article in the *Annales d'Hygiene Publique* (June, 1894) J. Voisin established as a matter of public record what a great many people already felt to be established by custom and observation: a statistically significant link between hairiness and idiocy.

*

BEAUTY

Beauty — a richly laden word — is the central issue in aesthetics. To the ancients, beauty was the external expression of internal virtue. Beauty had a moral character: ugly people are bad. But, of course, not only is beauty skin deep, it is notoriously fragile and elusive. Virgil says 'O, pretty boy, don't trust your looks'. In the medieval period beauty was construed to be an expression of the Divine. An old text by Albertus Magnus, but usually attributed to St Thomas Aquinas under the title *De Pulchro et Bono* (About Beauty and Goodness) contains the quintessential medieval definition of beauty:

A resplendence of form, whether in the duly-ordered parts of material objects, or in men, or in actions.

And beauty is culturally relative, an inspiration to a bewildering host of vegetable metaphors. Malays want women's cheeks to resemble a slice of mango and the nose a jasmine bud. The Japanese say a face should look like a melon seed. Old Testament Jews, according to *The Song of Songs*, wanted a women with a 'belly like a heap of wheat' and 'breasts like two fawns'. Arab authors praise blackness of hair and eyes, but the Troubadours want skin as white as milk. We call women we like 'honey'.

But all polemic is alive with wriggling half-truths. The fact is — in any era — ideals of beauty are *shared*, not imposed. Female beauty is the expression of the beliefs of an entire school of thought, not just the boys' dormitory. A common acceptance of aesthetic principles is one of the most telling expressions of any culture. Anthropologists believe that shared feelings about beauty arose from the Darwinian principles of selection, since being good looking in the sexual sense was a primary survival characteristic, but our real interest in beauty rests in the desire to take pleasure from other people's presence. In any age the search for beauty involves people of each sex trying to define what is generally pleasing.

The French have a saying that you must suffer to be beautiful. The '*beau laid* — beautiful ugly'.

BEER

Beer has always been uncouth, though it is structurally more complicated than wine. While grapes naturally contain tasty sugars and acids, the starches in the grains that make up beer are tasteless. Because it is such a powerful energy source and therefore voluminous and very filling, beer is an unsuitable accompaniment to food. Its use is therefore restricted to those bent on achieving a flatulent sort of stupefaction.

Beer was a by-product of bread in the ancient world. It has been argued that the discovery that mashed grain made a pleasing alcoholic drink was the source of agriculture itself. Baked bread was broken up in water and allowed to ferment for a day or so. This disgusting mixture became so popular that in Greek legend Dionysos fled Mesopotamia because the local population became too addicted and aggressive. In pre-Conquest Peru a form of beer was made by chewing ground corn and letting the natural enzymes in human spit transform the starch into glucose. This primitive beer, known as Chicha, has not (yet) been exported.

Despite its popularity in Germany and Tenerife, beer was not always an exclusively proletarian drink. In his engraving *Beer Street* William Hogarth (1697-1764) suggests that beer, as opposed to gin (the subject of his notorious print, *Gin Lane*), was a healthful, even luxurious commodity — the drink of the prosperous yeoman, not the downtrodden, rejected and despised urban poor. Beer's life-giving properties are also suggested by any number of eighteenth-century texts of which *The Compleat Housewife* (1753) is typical. This gives a recipe to promote fertility which contains strong ale, the spinal marrow of an ox, catmint, raisins, dates, nutmeg and orris. This might be the source of the claim made in *Cottage Economy* (1821) by

William Cobbett that the English were engaged in a process of slow national poisoning through beer, an opinion which remains no less valid today.

BICYCLES

Once a bold invention of Victorian manufacturing, then a proletarian prosthetic, now the bicycle has a renaissance of use and a fresh set of meanings. Independence, companionship, hard exercise and fresh air. The movement in the nineteenth century which united Bernard Shaw, Gustav Jaeger, Edward Carpenter, Hilaire Belloc, H.G. Wells and other Fabian-socialist-Christian utopians tended to move on two wheels. Unlike the perfumed, mannered *fin de siècle* posturing of Oscar Wilde (the man with a *green* carnation), Shaw, Carpenter and Belloc were energetically un-decadent. It is impossible to summon up an image of Oscar Wilde pedalling down Tite Street. To Shaw's circle the bicycle was a manifesto: a brilliant distillation of the laws of physics into a neat symbol of modern industrial civilisation.

BLACK

'Black' is lexicologically an extremely interesting word. The *Oxford English Dictionary* has forty-four columns of definition. In Old English there are two words tantalisingly close in spelling: *blaec* (meaning black) and *blac* (meaning pale). Blaec comes from the Teutonic *blakan*, meaning 'to burn'. American radical blacks now want, in a complex inversion of sensibilities, to be known as 'niggers'. In Latin, *niger* also meant 'bad' ... Curiously, this sense has been preserved (if distorted) in ghetto language where 'bad' means 'good', as in 'he is one bad ass' which, in fact, means he is rather a good egg.

An American writer of the 1840s could say, without irony, that 'the more pity I felt at the sight of this degraded and degenerate race the more ... impossible it becomes for me to repress the feeling that they are not of the same blood as we are'. E.A. Freeman, Regius Professor of Modern History at Oxford in 1884, said of the United States 'This would be a fine land if only every Irishman would kill a negro and be hanged for it'. He went on that blacks were 'hideous apes whom Darwin left unfinished.'

As Robert Penn Warren once pointed out, the danger in recognising the vast catalogue of injustice exercised on American blacks (now terminologically 'African-Americans') is a temptation towards sentimentality, or what James Baldwin called a 'protective sentimentality'. In his landmark book, *Notes of a Native Son* (1955), Martin Luther King was aware of this and once remarked 'You don't have to love me to stop lynching me'.

America's Noble Savage has been admired for his athletic prowess, his natural humour or for his soul, usually with a marked degree of (sometimes unconscious) condescension. In *The Subterraneans* Jack Kerouac has himself 'wishing I were a Negro, feeling that the best the white world had afforded was not enough ecstasy for me, not enough life, joy, kicks, darkness, music, not enough night'.

When he was preparing the manuscript of *Charlie and the Chocolate Factory* (1964), Roald Dahl had to agree that the Oompah-Loompahs were coloured orange so as to distance them from Afro-pygmies who were so clearly his model. Now research into the genetic character of IQ has to be pursued behind closed doors. A 1991 survey of black men in Baltimore between the ages of eighteen and thirty-five found that 56 per cent were either in prison, on probation or on parole. In 1994 Charles Murray (described by the windy *New York Times* as 'the most dangerous conservative in America') and Richard Herrnstein published their book *The Bell Curve: Intelligence and Class in American Life*. Based on research sponsored by the American Enterprise Institute in Washington, it argued the taboo that intelligence is largely inherited and that, therefore, crime has a root in race.

Considerable disquiet exists among white men about the apparent advantage which the black man enjoys in respect of the size of his penis. There is no sound scientific basis for this. The latest phalloplethysmographical research shows that the average black penis is, in fact, only a little longer than the white version. This issue is discussed at appropriate length in Ronald Hyam's *Empire and Sexuality: the British experience* (1991).

BORES

The malady of *ennui* is a result of the tragic human romance with knowledge. Voltaire says, in *Sept discours en vers sur l'homme* (1738), '*le secret d'ennuyer est de dire tout* – the success of boredom is to say all'. Ever since, economy has been a defining part of wit which might, itself, be described as the antidote to, or maybe just the opposite of, boredom itself. The gloomy religious polemicist Dean Inge said Joy was the opposite of Boredom.

It's a commonplace that sufferers from boredom are often people with high expectations and low tolerance of themselves, as much as of others. To Schopenhauer, just as necessity was the scourge of the working classes, so *ennui* was the scourge of the educated ones. Dean Inge said the experience of boredom was a sure sign that 'we are allowing our best faculties to rust in idleness'. Roland Barthes describes his own boredom at a dinner arising, he says, not out of the shortcomings of his hosts, but from his own uncertainty about how to communicate with them. He writes:

> I slid down the slope of silence; impossible to catch hold
> of anything: I grew bored because I looked bored. In
> other words, boredom is a kind of hysteria.

For A.A. Milne, author of *Winnie the Pooh*, there were two classes of bore; 'those who have their own particular subject and those who do not need a subject'. Coco Chanel sighed more existentially, 'Passion always goes ... boredom stays'.

The victim of a bore suffers tedium, a condition aptly defined by the cynical lexicographer Ambrose Bierce from the Latin mass *Te Deum Laudamus* in which 'apparently natural derivation' he said 'there is something that saddens'.

On the condition, John Updike observed that 'A healthy male adult bore consumes each year one and a half times his own weight in other people's patience' (*Assorted Prose*, 1965). It mainly occurs when someone is talking when you want to. Hence Ambrose Bierce defined a bore as 'a person who talks when you want him to listen'. You should always listen to the opinions of others. It won't do you any good, but it will them. Nonetheless—paraphrasing Dr Johnson—you should also never converse with someone who speaks more than he thinks. 'The habit of common and continuous speech is a symptom of mental deficiency. It proceeds from not knowing what is going on in other people's minds' Walter Bagehot said in his *Literary Studies* (1879).

Politicians know most about the subject and Henry Kissinger said: 'The advantage of being famous is that when you bore people, they think it's their fault.'

CARS

Along with advertising, movies and rock music, the car is one of the most distinctive cultural forms of the twentieth century, one that contains a good deal of the age's achievements, its longings and its bathos. The car is, according to the American satirist Sinclair Lewis (1885-1951), poetry and tragedy, love and heroism. A symbol of its age, the car as Roland Barthes (1915-80) remarked—not without irony—in his influential collection, *Mythologies* (1957), is our cathedral. The ecclesiastical metaphor is pursued by Martyn Goff in his novel, *The Youngest Director* (1984):

It was a glorious late autumn day in the age of the car.

Men worshipped the long or short, wide or narrow, high or low metal monsters as they had once worshipped God. Sunday was their day instead of His; they were the means of social introduction and interchange instead of His house; they had become the badge of rank instead of the pew in His church.

The car is perhaps the definitive consumer product, certainly it is the one in which the greatest amount of art, design, semantics and marketing genius is invested. At General Motors in the fifties, Harley Earl spoke of the 'dynamic economy', something Vance Packard later stigmatised as 'planned obsolescence'. A more charitable colleague of Earl's said of the corporation's annual model change 'We haven't depreciated these cars, we have appreciated your mind.'

The essence of the car's appeal can be found in Henry Ford's declaration that he had to invent the gasoline buggy to escape the mind-crushing tedium of life on a Midwest farm.

CELEBRITY

John Updike thinks celebrity is a mask that eats the face. It is as bad for business as it is for one's countenance. An American academic called Jim Collins found in a study of 1435 US corporations that there was a negative correlation between media exposure of the CEO and company performance.

CHAMPAGNE

Madame Bollinger explained: 'I drink it when I'm happy and when I'm sad. Sometimes I drink it when I'm alone. When I have company I consider it obligatory. I trifle with it if I'm not hungry and drink it when I am. Otherwise, I never touch it— unless I'm thirsty.' In 'La Côte Basque' (*Answered Prayers*, 1986) Truman Capote has a superb description of the taste of Roederer's Cristal, more recently the favourite tipple of gangsta rappers: 'A pale blaze, a chilled fire of such prickly dryness that, swallowed, seems not to have been swallowed at all, but instead to have been turned to vapours on the tongue and burned there to one damp sweet ash'.

CHANGE

'Nothing is permanent except change' was Heraclitus' view of the world, or one of them. This condition of continuous change is what defines cultural activity. The very word 'culture' suggests growth and evolution. In this constant progress there is, of course, also a sense of melancholy.

In his 1905 essay on infant sexuality, Freud explained that children, especially boys, get particular excitation from sensations of movement, possibly a source of the engine-driver fantasy young males have in the modern age. Speed is our most familiar experience of change and speed defines the twentieth-century experience.

Specialists in sport medicine understand the effects which velocity and, more important, rapid changes in velocity can have. Severe acceleration leads to a complete lack of vision (black-out), or restricted vision (grey-out).

On the way to black or grey, heart-rate always increases under the effect of positive g-loadings and researchers have found that racing drivers' pulses are often in the 160+ range. The normal rate is nearer 70. In acceleration — as blood pools in the legs — less is delivered to the heart and, what with one thing or another, you feel high.

Such is the fascination of speed that marketing men (and not just in the automobile industry) have made it their business to equate speed with success, thereby creating as a by-product one of the most enduring and least endearing myths of the century: the contribution of owning a fast car to personal aggregates of sexual activity.

*

CHIC

'Chic' — like *'la mode'*, *'avant-garde'* or *'retardataire'* — is a marvellous French term that untranslatably conveys a special meaning about material style or personal deportment. Literally, artistic skill and dexterity, it suggests unforced elegance, a natural inclination towards stylish grace. It is too hard to try and get it.

CLASS

Snobbery is a graduated conception of one's fellows, according to Oxford character Geoffrey Madan (who believed mere use of the words 'vision' and 'supremely' were infallible signs of the uneducated). Snobbery is a deprecatory synonym for distinction.

The old view was that 'There is not the slightest doubt that whatever tests of physical and mental proficiency are chosen, the children of the upper and middle classes are intrinsically far better endowed than the children of unskilled labourers'.

This opinion, which belongs to Dean Inge (*Wit and Wisdom*, 1927), attributes greater endowments to, say, an upper-class It-girl such as Tara Palmer-Tomkinson than the composer Ludwig van Beethoven.

CLASSICISM

To John Ruskin, classicism in architecture was not much better than the work of the devil. He described St Peter's, seat of the Vicar of Christ, as 'fit for nothing but a ballroom and it is a little too gaudy even for that'.

COCKTAIL

Cocktails are raffish. In John Galsworthy's *Forsyte Saga* we know that Montague Dartie is a cad, a spendthrift and generally unreliable when we find him indulging in a cocktail on that day in 1903 when Queen Victoria's funeral cortège passes his club.

Now the mood has changed, but cocktails retain a strong symbolic character: they are fixed in the Anglo-Saxon imagination as tokens of pleasure, celebration and gaiety.

The etymology of the word cocktail is curious. In the eighteenth century beer that was too fresh was known as a cocktail; this might in turn have its roots in the equine world. In stock-breeding, the term was applied to a horse of impure blood which is to say a mixture, almost an antonym of thoroughbred. Thoroughbreds had full tails, but these bastard beasts had their tails docked. A character in Thackeray says 'I can't afford a thoroughbred and hate a cocktail'.

By extension, cocktail suggested a man who was not quite a gentleman. Applied to a drink, the word may have a rather different source. There is a small, eccentric school which believes the word may derive from Xochitl, an Aztec princess who in pursuit of romance beguiled her king with a liquid concoction of her own invention (apparently with successful results). Perhaps less unlikely, in Bordeaux, a *coqutel* was a mixed drink and this term may have passed into English via French officers serving in Washington's Army in the American War of Independence.

In the contemporary sense cocktail first appeared in print in the United States in 1806 as the name of a mixed drink containing any spirit, sugar, water and bitters. By 1845 it was a published term: in Henry Didimus' *New Orleans as I Found It*, 'cocktail' describes brandy with bitters, drunk by the great *Times* journalist Sir William Howard Russell *before* breakfast.

The vogue for cocktails in the 1920s has often been described, but rarely analysed. Certainly, it was fundamental to the rehabilitation of gin. In his play, *The Cocktail Party* (1950), T.S. Eliot turns it into a mysterious rite. That they were such a delicious source of mockery for Evelyn Waugh is vivid proof of their popularity.

COFFEE

Drinking coffee is, according to modish Italian intellectual Piero Camporesi, 'an act of social promotion'.

Classical civilisation was based on wine and the Greeks invented a god to promote it. The Persian poets, too, write beguilingly of wine and its place in the theatre of love. But after the military and intellectual conquests of Islam, the Middle Eastern people were under firm encouragement to abandon drink. As a consequence, the status of coffee rose rapidly. Our word coffee derives from *kahweh*, Arabic for wine, but the effects of the two beverages are different: while alcohol is a narcotic which encourages sleep, coffee is a stimulant which encourages wakefulness.

According to Persian legend, Muhammed was one day in a state of unnatural somnolence when the Angel Gabriel came to him, offering relief with a brew, as black as the sacred Kaaba in Mecca. This was coffee, the 'wine of Islam', and from Muhammed's first sip we were endowed with a magical force unknown to antiquity.

The other account of the discovery of coffee is more prosaic, but perhaps more likely to have a basis in reality, since it concerns goat droppings. The French gastronomist Brillat-Savarin (1755-1826) said that coffee was discovered by a goatherd, who noticed 'a strange restlessness and hilarity in his flock whenever they browsed on coffee-berries.' Anthropologists might argue that it is the similarity between roast coffee-berries and goat dung that formed a bridge in our minds, giving rise to the fable. Brillat-Savarin also claimed that the 'extreme cerebral excitation' evident in Voltaire is attributable to his coffee addiction, a condition so extreme that Dumas described it as abuse.

Coffee is a socially acceptable drug, a powerful intoxicant. Our addiction can be attributed to the power of trimethyloxypurin, the active ingredient of caffeine, first isolated by a German chemist named Ferdinand Runge, in 1820. Trimethyloxypurin not only excites the familiar sense of ecstasy but also promotes peristalsis, diuresis and excites the respiratory centre of the *medulla oblongata* (brain stem). It also tends to remedy hangovers, contracting those very cranial arteries which alcohol so painfully expands.

CONCEPTUAL ART

Conceptual art was the invention of Marcel Duchamp, although he did not use the term. Duchamp was either a stylish, punning, enigmatic intellect or a mischievous fraud. It was Duchamp's 'ready-made' (the bottle drier, the urinal, the snow shovel) that laid the basis for acceptance of conceptual art today. Duchamp was dismissive of skill and finish, although he dodged the issue of whether a ready-made had to be on public display before it became art. 'It is not the idea of a work of art at all, it's the idea that it was chosen.'

The term may have been coined by American artist Sol Le Witt who believed 'the idea becomes a machine that makes the art'. Le Witt himself did not stay on high ground for long. By the early nineties he was designing perfume packaging.

An eloquent condemnation of conceptual art was Adolf Hitler's, who knew a few things on painting. At the opening of the infamous Degenerate Art Exhibition in Munich in 1937 Hitler said:

In this hour I affirm my unalterable resolve here, as in the realm of political confusion, to clear out all the claptrap from artistic life in Germany. 'Works of art' that are not capable of being understood in themselves but need some pretentious instruction book to justify their existence — until at long last they find someone sufficiently browbeaten to endure such stupid or impudent twaddle with patience — will never again find their way to the German people! ... From now on we are going to wage a merciless war of destruction against the last remaining elements of cultural disintegration.

The real problem with conceptual art is that the concepts are often so paltry.

CONSUMERISM

It is amusing that 'consume' was first used pejoratively, as when someone was consumed by disease or fire. Nowadays, consumerism is held in some quarters to be malign in itself, a symptom of the malaise of industrialised capitalist societies. Of course, the word itself has associations of waste and squandering as early as the fifteenth century. Only latterly French and German social scientists (consuming their word processors) have picked on the idea of consumption as a suitable area for obscurantist theorising.

The term was made current by pioneer social scientist, Beatrice Webb. A recent example of the mumbo-jumbo spoken of it comes from Jean Baudrillard, a French academic given to preparing diagrams showing the conceptual relationship between the early songs of Petula Clark and the Régie Autonome de Transports de Paris. Baudrillard writes, unforgettably:

The truth about consumption is that it is a *function of production* and not a function of pleasure ... [it] is the equivalent and the extension, in the twentieth century of the great indoctrination of rural populations into industrial labour, which occurred throughout the nineteenth century.

CONSERVATISM

The term conservative appeared originally in print in *The Quarterly Review* for January 1830 as a 'modern' alternative to the term Tory. Conservatism used to suggest an absolutely unfettered right for everyone to remain exactly where they were. To Ambrose Bierce a conservative was a statesman enamoured of existing evils, as opposed to a liberal who wishes to replace them with others.

It is often said, probably quite correctly, that we are all most conservative about the subjects we know best. By the same reasoning, it is often easy to be daringly original about a subject of which one is magnificently ignorant.

The paradox of the Conservative world-view was beautifully expressed by Lampedusa in *The Leopard*: 'If you want things to stay the same, they are going to have to change'.

CORNY

The expression 'corny' arose out of the prevalence of corn among the diet of simple countryfolk in the United States. By the early nineteenth century it had begun to acquire negative associations with poor rural whites and blacks and the simplistic wisdoms and hackneyed truths associated with them. There are records that Nebraskans were known as cornhuskers in the 1870s and soon after the word 'corn' began to suggest embarrassing sentiment or banality. Quite the opposite of originality, it may be the Anglo-American equivalent of the concept Flaubert found most trying about idiocy—though he would have found the term itself repugnant.

CRITICS

Only two qualifications are required of the critic: to be very intelligent and very well-informed. The combination is rare. Schopenhauer said you should treat a work of art like a prince and let it speak to you first. Critics exist to subvert this dignified process. They are the people Dr Johnson described as 'sentinels in the avenues of Fame'. There are five main types: the film critic, the literary critic, the television critic, the theatre critic and the art critic. Of these the film critic is the most pretentious, the literary critic the most captious, the television critic the most ridiculous, the theatre critic the most powerful and the art critic the most daunting.

To E.M. Forster, the activity of criticism was the very opposite of creativity. Not just in its inclination to destructiveness (by giving, as Dr Johnson had it, 'Ignorance and Envy the first notice of prey'), but as a fundamental process. Forster says 'Think before you speak is criticism's motto; speak before you think creation's' ('The Raison d'Etre of Criticism in the Arts' in *Two Cheers for Democracy*, 1951).

Some of the lasting value of criticism may be inferred from the following selection of comments on one great work by another great writer.

'An idiot' (H.L. Mencken on Henry James).

'Filth' (Joseph Conrad on D.H. Lawrence).

'Dull and commonplace' (*The Times* on The Gettysburg Address).

'What a good thing it isn't music' (Gioacchino Rossini on Felix Mendelssohn).

'This brown thing' (Claude Monet on J.M.W. Turner).

'Artificial flight is impossible' (Director of the US Naval Observatory in 1894).

Critical standards are inconstant. A French journalist retyped Marguerite Duras' award-winning *L'Après Midi de Monsieur Andesmas*, gave it another title and was delighted to have it rejected by all three of the great writer's publishing houses.

CONTROL

Overrated. According to Mario Andretti, if everything feels under control you are simply not going fast enough.

CREATIVITY

'Intelligence with an erection' was Victor Hugo's way of

defining imagination. Artistic creativity may be directly related to sexual frustration. In a letter to Liszt, Richard Wagner wrote 'Since I have never enjoyed in life the true happiness of love, I shall raise a monument to this most beautiful of all dreams, in which from beginning to end, this love shall for once be completely fulfilled.' Maybe a happy Wagner would have been less prolific. Diana Mosley, towards the end of her life, suggested that Mitford family friend Adolf Hitler might have been a less malign force had he been the beneficiary of a normal sex life.

Since Francis Bacon there has been a feeling that artistic or intellectual creativity may be related to (or in some cases a sublimation of) the natural urge to reproduce. In his *Essays* (1625) Bacon says creative people try 'to express the images of their minds, where those of their bodies have failed.' Similarly, Freud believed that a happy person never fantasises, that the source of creative thinking was unsatisfied wishes.

The creative personality is a notoriously difficult one. Creative artists have a reputation for carelessness or what they called *disprezzo* in the Renaissance. The creative person is also an egotist. In his introduction to *Don Quixote* Cervantes says that works of art must resemble their authors. Another characteristic is continuous restlessness and dissatisfaction. The Russian composer Shostakovich was always at work on his next work because he was so dissatisfied with the one he had just completed.

A psychiatrist, Dr Felix Post, explained that in the standard hierarchy of psychosis—which ranges from non-existent through mild to marked and then to severe—all the artists he examined in a 1994 survey were in the marked/severe area.

CUNT

Possibly from the Sanskrit for 'trench'. The French politician Clemenceau had an unsatisfactory meeting with his British equivalent Lloyd George, after which his aide said to him: '*Il est con, non*? – He is a cunt'. Clemenceau replied: '*Il n'a ni le charme, ni la profondeur* – He has neither its charm nor depth.'

CYNICISM

The word comes from the Greek for dog because the cynic who despises wealth and ease is supposed to have the aspect of a miserable hound. The cynics of Greece were founded by Antisthenes, but it was his follower Diogenes who is always associated with this unsettling school of philosophy: dogs-in-a-manger, given to woofing or sneering at wealth and ease. Diogenes himself chose to live in a barrel as a symbol of his disdain for worldly comforts. When the emperor Alexander the Great paid homage and visited the old man who lived in a tub he asked if there was anything he could do. Diogenes said 'yes, get out of my light'.

Pedantry was once defined (by a cynic) as more accuracy than the situation required. Cynics themselves have more despondency than the circumstances merit. They tend to anticipate future disappointments by entertaining a state of contemporary bitterness. Cynicism is often mistaken with scepticism, but the two should not be confused as there is a fundamental distinction: cynics hate the world, sceptics are merely distrustful of it.

DECONSTRUCTION

Deconstruction is an example of a counterfeit currency of thought, but one that has been influential among academics and critics of supposedly radical inclinations.

Most people, and only intelligent or unnaturally patient ones would even try, cannot get past page one of Jacques Derrida's *Of Grammatology* (1967), a classical Deconstructivist text. It literally defies comprehension and, therefore, the credulous are sometimes persuaded to attribute to it specially rich and profound meaning. Derrida is a self-styled philosopher, although it is remarkable that in such a hermetic discipline his work has had little influence within philosophy itself. Rather, he has been taken up most enthusiastically by less rigorous disciplines — film studies for instance, and literary criticism — where his pseudo-philosophical method is thought to add weight to an otherwise lightish subject. To real philosophers, Derrida's 'deconstruction' does not begin to approach necessary standards of intellectual clarity and methodological rigour.

It is a richly amusing paradox that the school of French thinkers who wanted to explicate, obfuscated. Deconstruction is related to phonocentrism, logocentrism, 'differance', 'puncept' and decentring, a process (of no proven value) which aims to analyse a text so as to deny it any central meaning. Deconstruction is dedicated to a semi-intelligible attack on reason. The nonsense of deconstruction is that, committed as it is to denying any conventional 'meaning' in a book (or what they pretentiously insist on calling a 'text'), they also deny any value or meaning in their own critical methods.

Deconstructionism was amusingly defined by Morris Zapp, David Lodge's lovable professor of literature at Euphoria State University, in his novel *Small World* (1984). 'I'm a bit of a deconstructionist myself', says Zapp, 'It's kind of exciting — the last intellectuals.'

A prologue to the discrediting of Paul De Man as an anti-semitic bigot came with the bizarre events of the later life of the deluded yet modish ideologue Louis Althusser (1918-1990), author of *Pour Marx* (1965), *Lire 'Le Capital'* (1965) and a hundred psychoanalytically inspired late interpretations of Marx, all wearily abstract. It was Althusser's stock-in-trade at Paris Ecole Normale Superieure (where he was conventionally employed as a salaried revolutionary) to peddle bafflingly dense and allusive theory whose very resistance to interpretation was taken as a proof of special validity.

In his indulgently confessional and boastful autobiography, *L'Avenir dure longtemps* (The future lasts a long time, 1992) Louis Althusser describes running into the courtyard of the Ecole one winter morning in 1980, shouting that he had just killed his wife. Before the police arrived he was taken off to a mental hospital where he remained until his death. In his last book he describes himself as a 'trickster and a deceiver'.

DECORATION

According to the Marxist historian Eric Hobsbawm, the less sophisticated the mass public, the greater the appeal of decoration.

DEPRESSION

Anger without enthusiasm.

DIETING

In Roland Barthes' interview with French *Playboy*, 'The Shape I'm In', he discusses the phenomenon of losing weight and its mythology. He regards it as a 'religious neurosis' and makes the following comparison;

> Going on a diet has all the characteristics of a conversion. With all the same problems of lapsing, and then returning to the conversion. With certain books that are like gospels, etc. a diet mobilises an acute sense of wrongdoing, something which threatens, which is there every minute of the day. It is only when you sleep that you are sure of not doing something wrong. From the moment you accept the rules of the diet, whether it is 'low calorie' or 'sugar free', since the rules are very strict, there are … a thousand failures.

He points out how we 'hallucinate' by 'feeling' fatter an hour after eating 10 grammes of sugar although we don't actually gain weight from it for at least 24-48 hours.

Barthes believes the central question of dieting is one of maintenance—finding a way of eating that you won't think about any more. He illustrates the difficulty of doing this by relating to *Playboy* a conversation he had with the administrator of the prestigious Collège de France, during his first visit for candidature, about the American statistics on the percentage of successful weight-loss diets:

Barely 5% last—the others last a while, then they give up.

In the modern world, there is a social dialectic which keeps you from sticking to a diet: if you eat something with someone, you are immediately subjected to the other's attention, which keeps you from respecting your diet in one way or another.

DRINK

Dylan Thomas' definition of an alcoholic is someone you don't like and who drinks as much as you do.

Alcohol is a stimulant, a narcotic and a beverage. It is distinguished from other recreational drugs in that it has nutritional properties. It is distinguished from vitamins in that, in some of its forms, it has complex and satisfying aesthetic qualities which to appreciate properly, require a disciplined and well-trained mind.

Alcohol alters consciousness. The taste for altering consciousness is so nearly universal that it is tempting to regard it as instinctive, even 'natural'. In Siberia they ferment red algae; American Indians, maple syrup; Central American Indians, agave and cactus; South American Indians; jungle fruits; Asians rice; Europeans grapes and grain. The names which distilled spirits attract are witness to their universality: Aqua vitae, Eau de vie, Akvavit, Uisge beatha (whiskey).

Man's primary biological needs are body-bound: hunger, thirst, sex. His secondary needs are spiritual: religion and art. Alcoholic drink powerfully unites the two appetites. The respect for alcohol in history is profound and revealing. In Byzantium the Emperor and the Patriarch went to the vineyards every 19th August and consecrated the grapes with full liturgical procedure. In the sixth century there was a Frankish legal code called the *lex salica* which put winegrowers under special protection.

Alcohol has been fundamental to the development of our civilisation. Professor George Saintsbury, author of *Notes on a Cellar Book* (1920), said:

> There is absolutely no scientific proof, of a trustworthy kind, that moderate consumption of sound alcoholic liquor does a healthy body any harm at all; while on the other hand it is the unbroken testimony of all history that alcoholic liquors have been used by the strongest, wisest, handsomest and in every way best races of all times.

Tolstoy's essay 'Why Do Men Stupefy Themselves?' was written *de haut en bas* and very specifically from the Russian point of view. He says:

> The cause of the worldwide consumption of hashish, opium, wine, and tobacco lies not in the taste nor in any pleasure, recreation or fun they afford, but simply in man's need to hide from himself the demands of conscience … for man is a spiritual as well as animal being. He may be moved by things that influence his spiritual nature, or by things that influence his animal nature.

In any discussion of alcohol use and abuse it is necessary to distinguish between the brutish desire to stupefy with industrial alcohol and the more refined pleasures of serious drinking. The almost indescribable complexity of, say, a first-growth claret, or the intense depth and flavour of one of the great old Romanée Conti Burgundies, are genuine aesthetic experiences.

There is an incidence so high in the drink-creativity relationship that it is tempting to see a direct connection. Of the seven native-born American Nobel laureates, five—Sinclair Lewis, Eugene O'Neill, William Faulkner, Ernest Hemingway and John Steinbeck—were alcoholics. O'Neill simply couldn't get out of bed unless he had drunk a quart of gin. Many writers have testified to their creative dependence on alcohol. To some it seems to be a sort of witchdoctory, a type of self-medication. Faulkner said, perhaps unaware of the medical inference,

There ain't nothing I got whiskey won't cure.

The best account of the creative writer's relationship with alcohol is William Styron's.

Like a great many American writers, whose sometimes lethal addiction to alcohol has become so legendary as to provide in itself a stream of studies and books, I used alcohol as the enhancement of the imagination. There is no need to either rue or apologise for my use of this soothing, often sublime, agent, which had contributed greatly to my writing: although I never set down a line under its influence, I did use it—often in conjunction with music—as a means to let my mind conceive visions that the unaltered, sober brain has no access to. Alcohol was an invaluable senior partner of my intellect, besides being a friend whose ministrations I sought daily.

Writers are preoccupied by changing consciousness and changing states. F. Scott Fitzgerald wrote in 1918 (before his eventual decline) that:

I was never disposed to accept the present but always striving to change it, better it, or even sometimes to destroy it. There were always far horizons that were more golden, bluer skies somewhere.

Alcohol famously changes one's perception of time. People drink because they are bored. 'No man is happy in the present, unless drunk' said Dr Johnson. Time never hangs on your hands with a drink. In this attitude to time is the deeper truth behind the creative artist's addiction to drink.

Zoologists only study animals up to the point when their reproductive obligations are fulfilled and neglect the later years which are viewed as periods of decline, rather than of stability or maturity. The metaphor of writing and giving birth is relevant here. Drink appears to obviate the 'drying-up' which creative people fear. Looking at American writers it is noteworthy how many of them peaked in their forties, precisely when their really heavy drinking began. Fitzgerald's best work was finished with the publication of *Tender is the Night* when he was thirty-eight. Hemingway's last good book was *For Whom the Bell Tolls*, published when he was forty-one. Faulkner's *Go Down Moses* appeared when he was forty-four.

It used to be thought that optimum performance in intelligence tests occurred at the age of sixteen. All Isaac Newton's major discoveries were made by the time he was twenty-four. No major advance in mathematics has been made by a man over fifty. It also disrupts the fearsome rush of Time. Drink appears to forestall the encounter with death.

EGOTISM

To Ambrose Bierce an egotist was 'a person of low taste, more interested in himself than me.'

EROTICISM

Eroticism is a specialised attitude to human reproductive activity. It is sex, or the contemplation of sex, developed from a survival characteristic into a cultivated pleasure.

In his difficult book *Eroticism* (1957), Georges Bataille argues that the erotic impulse underlies all religion and philosophy since discretionary coupling (or the contemplation of it) is a mechanical way of breaching the appalling abyss which is each individual's singular loneliness. Philosophy and religion translate the spasm of the groin into the world of ideas. The notion of sexuality being fundamental to human activity goes back to before Bataille and beyond Freud. In his essay *On Women* Arthur Schopenhauer mocked the male's obsession with women's bodies:

> Only a male intellect clouded by the sexual drive could call the stunted, narrow-shouldered, broad-hipped and short-legged sex the fair sex.

Eroticism is a considerable source of art and literature, although much erotic art is second-rate. But it is not to be confused with pornography. Maurice Girodias, the Jewish Mancunian who founded Paris' Olympia Press and published Samuel Beckett and Vladimir Nabokov as well as a great deal of filth, said, in an essay called 'More Heat than Light', that there was only good writing and bad.

EVIL

There is a splendid description of Satan in The Earl of Northampton's *A Defensative against the Poyson of Supposed Prophecies* (1583): 'His favours are but fancies and make no man fat; his glory like a stayned robe which can give no dignity; his service as a net to catch the wind'.

EVOLUTION

Occurred because God was disappointed in monkeys.

FASHION

The arsenic of pride, the business of buying stuff you do not need with money you have not got to impress people you do not like.

Fashion is simply what is done. What Robert Louis Stevenson did was wear a black flannel shirt, a knitted tie twisted into a knot, wellington boots, tight dark trousers, a pea -green jacket, white sombrero and a lady's sealskin cape fastened at the neck by a family brooch held together by a bunch of daffodils. Montaigne saw women swallow gravel, ashes, coals, dust, tallow, candles 'to get a pale-bleak colour. To become slender in waist, and to have a straight spagnolised body.' All attempts to systematise fashion have failed. Roland Barthes in *The Fashion System* serves only to make more obscure that which he had intended to clarify.

The vagaries of fashion are revealed in the etymology of related words. 'Vogue' comes from the Old French *voguer* meaning to sail forth. 'Haughty, trifling, affected servile, despotic, mean and ambitious.' That list is William Hazlitt's, but it is as relevant a description of fashion now as fashion one hundred and fifty years ago.

FEMINISM

'One needs' Arthur Schopenhauer wrote in his essay *On Women* 'only to see the way she is built to realise that woman is not intended for great mental or for great physical labour.' They are, he says 'childish, silly and short-sighted.'

'Women', once defined as the unfair sex, 'can be taught not to talk', according to Ambrose Bierce, but this would retard civilisation. There are legions of politically incorrect observations on women, one of the most dramatic being Dr Johnson's: 'Nature has given women so much power that the law has very wisely given them little.'

The absurdity of the feminist case is taken to its most extreme in academic texts. The terrible poverty of feminist thinking is well illustrated in the strangulated prose and pseudo-intellectual mumbo-jumbo favoured by academic specialists in the subject. Shannon Bell's *Reading, Writing, and Re-Writing the Prostitute Body* is typical of the genre. A blurb helpfully explains: 'a fascinating book: wide-ranging, readable.' Bell shows how the flesh and blood female body engaged in sexual interaction for payment has no inherent meaning and is signified differently in different cultures or discourses. The author contends that modernity has produced 'the prostitute' as the other within the categorial other woman.

FLYING

There are only two emotions involved in flying: fear and boredom, at least in the opinion of Orson Welles. Although flying has become commonplace, it still excites some primitive fears. For instance, even among those familiar with air travel it is notable how much more jaunty people are when getting *off* rather than getting on a plane.

Jet travel is a consumerised package that realises the modernist dream of technology's ability to change life for the better: a CFM56 turbine and a 737 airframe turn men into angels. Flight has in fact been only a mediocre source of inspiration for artists and writers. The only great literature produced by flight has been that of Antoine de St-Exupery whose sweet fable *The Little Prince* (written in New York at the beginning of the Second World War) has become the best-selling French book. It is significant that St-Exupery's inspiration was that the experience of flight is a reminder of the excitements of child-like innocence in the face of the world and its troubles: since his boyhood, St-Exupery had been deeply troubled by the loss of his ancient family home near Lyon. To this aristocratic Frenchman, flight was a catharsis. To Americans flight was also profoundly romantic, but it was a romance of a different sort, one that reaffirmed the dynamism and heroism of a nation populated by Amelia Earhart and Charles Lindbergh. This sense of triumphalist wonder has remained with the writer and critic, Gore Vidal, a pioneer passenger, whose father, Eugene L. Vidal, was appointed Director of the Bureau of Air Commerce by Franklin D. Roosevelt.

St-Exupery disappeared in 1944 when returning to Corsica from a reconnaissance mission up the Rhône Valley. It is speculated that, had he not taken a nostalgic diversion to overfly his mother's house, he might not have met the German fighters who probably shot him down. Another body that has never been found is Amelia Earhart's. Perhaps suffering from a difficult early menopause, she had declared that she wanted to fly off to a desert island and stay there. She disappeared during her 1936 round-the-world trip. There were subsequently many sightings of a white woman on desert islands. The most fascinating of these came from a Russian sailor who saw such a woman wearing jockey shorts. It had certainly been her habit to sport men's underwear in-flight, but her manager, assuming her loyalty would be to him, could not confirm the sighting since his own preference was for boxer shorts. Eugene Vidal never told him that Ms. Earheart had for some time been using his own Y-fronts.

FRENCH

'How can you be expected to govern a country that has two hundred and forty-six kinds of cheese?' Charles De Gaulle asked a *Newsweek* reporter in 1962. 'Love France, hate the French' is a maxim frequently invoked by Englishmen at a loss to understand the contrary allure of the neighbouring culture. France is a totality, much more so than Britain. Of course, the French have as many social classes as we do, but the difference is that the French class system is cohesive rather than divisive.

But admiration is not universal. The *mondain* George Santayana wrote:

[Paris] ... did very well for an occasional season of cosmopolitan pleasures, but even its intellectual and artistic movements, though they greatly attracted and rewarded attention, were episodes, fashions, and extravagances with which no one would wish to be identified. Even distinguished and philosophical persons I came across never inspired any confidence in my mind ... [since] ... none of them was a Catholic, so

that in all of them there was a certain strain of self-
consciousness, as of outsiders who always felt a little
aggrieved and a little insincere in the French
atmosphere. I have never had a French friend. In the
most charming of them I felt something false, as if an
evil spell bound them to some secret and sinister cause,
and they were feigning all their amiability for an
ulterior reason. They could never be disinterested,
never detached. They had in their hearts a sort of covert
intensity and stubborn nearsightedness that I could not
endure … The French mind is an exquisite medium for
conveying such things as can be communicated in
words. It is the unspoken things of which one feels the
absence or mistrusts the quality.

My Host the World, 1953.

The English have journeyed through real and imaginary France
maintaining visions that are precious and distinctive. The
France of loveable, but cunning, peasants, of fantasy breakfasts,
lunches, colourful markets, dappled sunshine and savour is no
less profound because it is not entirely real. The topography of
the countries we construct in the imagination speaks volumes
about our own: the love of France which made Peter Mayle a
bestseller is a recent novelty. France, as readers of Smollett and
Sterne know, was once regarded as risibly dirty and
backward—the French as skulking schemers or dessicated,
perfumed, high-minded cheats. At Marquise, just outside
Calais, Lord Nelson was

… shown an inn—they called it—I should have called it
a pigsty: we were shown into a room with two straw
beds, and, with great difficulty, they mustered-up clean
sheets, and gave us two pigeons for supper, upon a dirty
cloth, and wooden-handled knives. O what a transition
from happy England!

Today, France represents what we have lost. In particular,

this huge, uncrowded country has a pastoral life which is almost real. It has, or so it seems, traditions of cooking and hospitality which are ignorant of portion control and dedicated to pleasure as much as to nutrition and shelter. It has a national style which is borne of natural convictions, not of concepts fabricated by some wally from the Tourist Authority. See a picturesque French village and, if you are lucky, there will be someone there who smokes ham, a farmer who makes cheese, a baker who bakes bread. See an equally picturesque English village and you just sit it out and wait for the Walls, Dairy Crest and Mother's Pride trucks.

Food is the most complete expression of French style. 'Mayonnaise' according to Ambrose Bierce, is 'one of the sauces which serve the French in place of a state religion.'

It is not just because we find their food delicious that we revere France, but because the attention to food suggests sympathy for day-to-day human endeavour: a respect for normalcy is the basis of the real French style and this is shared by all classes. In *The Alice B. Toklas Cookbook* (1954), Gertrude Stein's famous companion writes:

> The French approach to food is characteristic; they bring to their consideration of the table the same appreciation, respect, intelligence and lively interest they have for the other arts ... I have heard working men in Paris discuss the way their wives prepare a beef stew as it is cooked in Burgundy, or the way a cabbage is cooked with salt pork and browned in the oven.

In his *Manual of Diet in Health and Disease* (1875) Thomas King Chambers wrote

> It is impossible to avoid the greasy dishes which are apparently preferred by all except our own countrymen; and a frequent consequence is rancid indigestion, with a

> nauseous taste in the mouth, and flatulence or diarrhoea
> … Another article that offends the bowels of unused
> Britons is garlic … flatulence and looseness are the
> frequent results.

French style is like a bidet, something at once odd, but also very convenient. A frank acknowledgement of practical human failings, but at the same time a source of keen pleasure in remedying them.

FUCK

Fuck—a robust term—is perhaps the most powerful word in the English language. It is the subject of a lexicological monograph by Jesse Sheidlower whose *The F Word* was published in 1995. Although familiar, it still has the dash of daring about it and, used sparingly, can halt conversations. One adventurous explanation of its origins appears in James Barke's *Pornography and Bawdy in Literature and Society* (1959) where he says it is a word onomatopoeic in origin, replicating the sound made by a penis in a vagina. There is a more linguistically precise account. Etymologically, it is from the French *foûtre* and related to German *ficken* (to strike). Old Norse *fukja* means to drive, a sense preserved in the Scots nautical expression fucksail (foresail) and the Dutch *fokzijl*. The idea of strokes is retained in English: bang, knock, bonk. The sense of action and weaponry is preserved in chopper. 'Screw' comes from Latin *scrofa*, meaning sow which became confused with another Latin word, *scrobis*, meaning ditch, which was a vulgar word for the vulva. An older form was 'swive' which survived in parallel, but has now vanished.

Scholars debate the first appearance of the word in print. It appears in William Dunbar's *A Bout of Wooing* (circa 1503), but as this was written in dense Scottish, it escaped the censors. F**k first appeared in Francis Grose's *Classical Dictionary of the Vulgar Tongue* (1785). Only in 1959 was the word first used in a respectable publication, Grove Press' unexpurgated edition of D.H. Lawrence's *Lady Chatterley's Lover* (this at a time when the Lord Chamberlain insisted to the playwright John Osborne that he could not use the expression 'piss off' and had to replace it with 'shut your steaming gob').

Fuck has extended grammatically from a Late Middle English verb to every part of speech. The copulatory verb is the most familiar swear word. In *A Worlde of Wordes* (1598), John Florio offers the Elizabethan range of synonyms: 'to iape, to sard, to fucke, to swive, to occupy.' By some estimates there are more than 1200 contemporary synonyms. The euphemism 'four-letter-word' appeared in 1934. The first modern reference book to include the word was Sir William A. Craigie's *Dictionary of the Older Scottish Tongue* (1938, 1951) which also includes the interesting expression 'cunt-laird' although, curiously, adds that its meaning is 'obscure'.

Fuck is an expletive and fucking an intensifier which have eventually acquired extended meanings. To fuck up is not to enjoy sexual actvity, but to get something badly wrong. A select subspecies of acronyms has evolved from this. SNAFU is 'situation normal: all fucked-up' used, according to Eric Partridge in his *Dictionary of Slang and Unconventional English* (1961), by the Army in the forties. Variations include FUBAR for 'fucked-up beyond all recognition' and SAPFU 'surpassing all previous fuck-ups.' A woman enamoured of sex is said to be 'fuck struck.' The competitive social circumstances in the hour before pubs and clubs close is now known as the 'fuck rush'.

FUNERALS

Apart from moving house, a funeral is the most distressing function of contemporary life. Richard Curtis, author of the successful movie *Four Weddings and a Funeral*, explained that in the United States the distributors wanted to change the title to *Toffs on Heat* on account of the dire forebodings implied in the original. We get the word from Latin. Funeral seems to come from *funeralis*, the adjective describing a burial, or *funus* which in turn seems to come from *fumus*, for smoke suggesting the popularity of cremations amongst the Romans who conducted their burials at night so the officials would not be polluted and defiled by the sight of the corpse.

Most of our funeral customs derive from the Romans, as: dressing in black, walking in procession, carrying insignia on the bier, raising a mound in the grave (called *tumulus*, whence our word tomb). The Greeks crowned the dead body with flowers, and also placed flowers on the tomb and the Romans had similar customs. Funeral ceremonies have always been trying, not just on account of grief: as La Rochefoucauld remarked, they tend to tell you more about the vanity of the living than the dead.

Despite its classical origins, the modern funeral and its attendant rites were, like so many other 'traditions', established as social procedure in the nineteenth century. The commercialisation of the toilette of the grave was just the most permanent aspect of a century that secularised death. The great municipal cemeteries of London and Paris were necessary in a functional as well as a ceremonial sense. With the shift of population from the country to the city, simple burial in a churchyard was no longer possible or practical. An industry was established to cope with it. Some found this distasteful. When Villiers de l'Isle Adam (author of the play *Axel*, where a character says 'Living! Who cares about living? Our servants can do that for us') was walking past the flower sellers and monumental masons outside Paris' Père Lachaise cemetery he once angrily remarked, 'Those are the people who invented death!'

The secularisation of death led to considerable aesthetic elaboration in the funeral artefacts. Our expression 'with knobs on' to suggest something tiresomely fancy comes from the practice of adding frivolous embellishments to Victorian coffins, a practice which reached its absurd peak in the United States during the sixties. In her hilarious book *The American Way of Death* (1963), Jessica Mitford describes a casket known as The Colonial Classic Beauty, intended to turn the toilette of the grave into an overstuffed lounge.

Funeral practices are not universally the same. The Koryaks of north-eastern Siberia play cards on corpses. In India Jains leave cadavers on exposed slabs in the open air so that carnivorous birds can recycle the deceased, while the Melanesians enjoy the practice of sarco[flesh]-cannibalism. To Bronislaw Malinowski, the great Polish anthropologist who studied death rites, this custom of eating the flesh of the recently dead was a supreme act of love and piety (*Science, Religion and Reality*, 1925). Although we know from Sophocles that interment was sanctioned by the gods, cremations have been preferred by forward thinkers at least since the seventeenth century when Sir Thomas Browne wrote his critical commentary, *Urn Burial* (1736). Browne warns against the dangers of burying dead bodies whole and entire: 'To be knaved out of our graves, to have our skulls made drinking-bowls, and our bones turned into pipes, to delight and port our Enemies, are tragical abominations escaped in burning burials.'

In modern town-planning theory there has been a reaction against the vast nineteenth-century cemeteries (although in Paris at Montmartre, Montparnasse and Père Lachaise it has to be admitted that there is nothing solemn or gloomy about these museums of dead Frenchmen). The influential architectural polemicist from Berkeley, Christopher Alexander, argued in his book *A Pattern Language* (1977) that cemeteries should be small, local and intimate rather than huge, metropolitan and impersonal. This is exactly how they are in southern Italy. In Positano, on the Amalfi coast, the troglodytic cemetery high above the town is a source of wonder and beauty, especially at night when each tomb is candle-lit. It is as if the southern Italians have preserved that sense of agreeable wonder about death that D.H. Lawrence imagined belonging to their predecessors, the Etruscans. In *Etruscan Places* Lawrence says that to these early inhabitants of central Italy, death was 'a pleasant continuance of life.' Today we find it hard to maintain this optimistic death-enhancing approach, hence the business of the funeral which, to Tennessee Williams, in *A Streetcar Named Desire* (1947) was 'pretty compared to death.'

GAY

Justinian believed sodomy caused earthquakes, a theory not yet disproven. Gay is, of course, a terrible misnomer. Arthur Schlesinger said it 'used to be one of the most agreeable words in the language' and 'Its appropriation by a notably morose group is an act of piracy.' Chaucer used the expression 'gay girls' to describe sexually active women.

The term homosexual was coined in 1869 by a Hungarian physician called Benkert, although it was popularised by Richard von Krafft-Ebbing in *Psychopathia Sexualis* (1886), the book most often stolen from public libraries.

There was, before the currency of the word 'gay' in the sixties (especially by the Gay Liberation Front) in the history of modern homosexuality, a consistent trend towards the 'decent obscurity of a learned language' with the pseudo-classical terms: paederast, ganymede, pathic, catamite, sodomite, for male homosexuality, lesbian and Sapphist for female. This taste for obscurity might be more easily understood if it is explained that as late as 1889, *The Birmingham Daily Post* described homosexuality as a 'hideous and foetid gangrene.'

Although recent surveys tend to show a growing tolerance of homosexuality, it has excited fears and inhibitions since Biblical times. 'If a man also lie with a man, as he lieth with a woman, both of them have committed an abomination; they shall surely be put to death.' Margaret Mead, who, as the author of numerous serious academic works, could draw on a cornucopia of anthropological knowledge (rather than upon a bunch of convictions acquired while pleasurably cruising Manhattan leather bars), believed 'extreme homosexuality is a perversion.'

Only since 1978 has homosexuality been dropped from the American Psychiatric Association's approved list of psychiatric neuroses (although some backward countries still diagnose it as a form of 'sluggish schizophrenia' and in Iran it is punishable by death, while it is still illegal in many of the United States and the *Soviet Medical Encyclopaedia* did not have an entry for 'lesbianism'). It is now politically correct to regard it as a mere erotic preference, although physiological explanations continue to mutate. They include: biochemical propositions, genetic predisposition, endocrinological disorders, oedipal junk and complications arising out of autoerotic narcissism. In 1991 Dr Simon LeVay, a British neurologist at San Diego's Salk Institute, reported in the reputable journal *Science* that the actual brain structure of gay men was different from the one of men who preferred sex with women. In heterosexual males, a node of the hypothalamus (which has a precise role in sexual behaviour) is sometimes three times larger than in gays. When these nodes are damaged in male monkeys, the sexual drive is unchanged, but is less distinctly heterosexual. The anatomical form of this tiny node is similar in women and in male homosexuals, giving a physiological basis for accusations of 'effeminacy.'

The modern condition of gayness with all its colourful attributes is an invention of New York. On 20th June 1994 *New York* magazine ran a cover story 'Is Everybody Gay?' The city has something of a tradition in this area. Lord Cornbury, Queen Anne's Governor of New York from 1702 to 1708, was a notorious transvestite. He explained:

You are very stupid not to see the propriety of it ... I represent a woman, and ought in all respects to represent her as faithfully as I can.

GERMANS

Early Americans debated whether English or Platt-Deutsch should become the official language of the United States. Mark Twain found the German language a source of amusement. 'Whenever the literary German dives into a sentence, that is the last you are going to see of him till he emerges on the other side of the Atlantic with his verb in his mouth.' He added that German humour is no laughing matter.

The Germans have a reputation for being good at cars, philosophy, classical music and applied science, but awful at everything else. Charles V said he spoke French to his mistress, Italian to his courtier and German to his horse, although the Duke of Windsor broke with tradition and used German when speaking to his staff during French exile. The historian A.J.P. Taylor once remarked 'What is wrong with Germany is that there is too much of it.'

German crassness is a staple of European literature. Montaigne admired the crudity of German drinking habits: 'The Germans enjoy drinking virtually any wine. Their habit is to gulp it rather than to taste it. They get a better bargain.' Nietzsche described his fellow countrymen as 'ponderous, viscous, and solemnly clumsy ... long-winded and boring.'

The German expression for 'tearing one's hair' is, accordingly, '*Eigeneshaarsichauszupflückenplage.*'

GLASSES

'Men' according to Dorothy Parker 'seldom make passes at girls who wear glasses.' There is still some residual stigma attached to glasses, but less than to an orthopaedic boot. Like all nostrums reconciling design and manners, Dorothy Parker's is no more than a half truth. One of the most seductive images is the woman in dark glasses: is it the mystery that fascinates or the extrovert dedication to effect that arouses? Certainly, glasses are saying something: Germans of the old school actively encouraged the monocle ('*Einglas*') since they believed it demanded discipline and muscular control of the wearer, characteristics then deemed to be fashionable.

But if popular culture tends to stress that women in glasses are disadvantaged, then it also maintains that men in glasses are wimps. The last photograph taken of Saddam Hussein had him wearing glasses and this was interpreted as a sign of his failing power(s).

Yet historically, glasses have more often been associated with positive status than with negative. In Spain the actual size of the lenses conferred prestige on the wearer. El Greco's magnificent, harrowing 1596 portrait of *Cardinal Nino de Guevara* shows God's representative in glowering glasses: the possession of such technology spoke eloquently about the power and tastes of the wearer.

Although the basic concept of glasses has now reached a steady state, it took more than three hundred years to develop the fundamental design of rigid sidepieces and a lens in front of each eye: Seneca used to peer through a bowl of water to achieve magnification and the first definition of 'spectacle', in an Italian tract of 1289, was as a lens with a frame and a handle, something to hold, not to *wear*. Here there were no fashion implications. Later, leather thongs—or even clips—were used to attach the frame to the neck or the temple. Early glasses had a hinge to grip the nose where we now expect a fixed bridge.

It was the invention of printing and the creation of a mass market for books that increased demand for glasses. Samuel Pepys tried to read through tubes before he realised that lenses 'promised very great ease.' Technically, the form of the frame has been stable since the eighteenth century: well-known self-portraits by Chardin and Joshua Reynolds show glasses that could be worn today. But this technical stability encourages extraordinary experimentation: the contemporary range of shapes, styles, colours and the occasional meretricious *gaucherie* is genuinely astonishing.

The history of glasses shows how prosthetic devices can evolve into fashion accessories, as if there is an ineluctable human drive to make even surgical devices the basis for competition in matters of style. Frames made out of precious, or merely attractive materials, gold, silver, chrome or horn, are natural candidates for this transformation into jewellery, but the significant human point is that maybe there is real potential for other presently stigmatised medical devices to come out of the clinic and onto the streets. With glasses the principle of acceptable transformation has been established.

HEDONISM

Ingrid Bergman said good health and a bad memory are prerequisites for happiness. '*Timor mortis conturbat me*' — the dread of death overwhelms me — that dreadful refrain from William Dunbar's *Lament for the Makers* is the surest antidote to complacency, since the prospect of death is a sauce which simultaneously enhances and diminishes our enjoyment of what life dishes up. Hedonism is denial of mortality. Epicurus, in his celebrated *Letter to Menoeceus,* has better news for those bent on pleasure.

So death, the most terrifying of ills, is nothing to us, since so long as we exist, death is not with us; but when death comes, then we do not exist. It does not then concern either the living or the dead, since for the former it is not, and the latter are no more.

The idea of hedonism is related to time, a melancholy fugitive quality. Roland Barthes was fascinated by the gourmet Brillat-Savarin, author of *La Physiologie du gout* (1828). He noted that, like all hedonists, Brillat-Savarin also had a keen sense of boredom. Everything—especially the taste of food—which 'arises from an initial temporality is endowed with a sort of enchantment.'

HERITAGE

Love of the past: English disease. Dr Johnson recognised this: 'The time present is seldom able to fill desire or imagination with immediate enjoyment, and we are forced to supply its deficiencies by recollection or anticipation.'

INSULTS

An insult is to jump on people (from the Latin *in*, upon, and *salire*, to leap). Today we tend to leap on people with four-letter words, with one or two fingers. A famous modern insult is Alan Clark's comment that Michael Heseltine looks like the sort of man who bought his own furniture. Freud quoted an anonymous English author who said 'the man who first flung a word of abuse at his enemy instead of a spear was the founder of civilisation.'

The commonplace that four-letter words are Anglo-Saxon is only a half truth. In fact, only shit, arse and turd are genuinely Anglo-Saxon. The etymology of fuck and cunt, despite the robust Anglo-Saxon sound, is in fact uncertain. Cunt appears in Middle English circa 1200 and has lots of cognate forms: Old Norse *kunta*, Dutch *kut* all deriving from latin *cunneus*, a wedge. This goes into French as *con* and Italian as *conno*. (Here it is irresistible to mention that etymologically vanilla and vagina have the same origins.)

Crap is very modern, possibly coming from Thomas Crapper's patent valveless Water Waste Preventer (the plumber invented by Wallace Reyburn, 1913-2001). Withal, obscene language is variable in its ability to cause offence. The very fact that the *Oxford English Dictionary* says some words are not 'now in polite use' immediately suggests that they once were. In his *Dictionary*, Samuel Johnson lists a flower known as arse-smart.

The source of medieval insults was religion. Later, xenophobia took over, something which has continued into our own century. A defendant in Middlesex courts in 1915 said 'He called me a German and other filthy names!' The following list gives something of the rich flavour and range of reference in the xenophobic insult. Jew, kaffir, nigger, frog, greaser, gringo, sambo, Jap, yid, mick, limey, kike, chink, wop, boche, fritz, hun, jerry, kraut, pom, wog, spick, eyetie, wetback, nip, gook, slant, honkie, paki.

But today, overwhelmingly, insults are based on sex. The source of sexual insults, according to D.H. Lawrence, was the horror of sexual life brought about by the sixteenth-century plague of syphilis. While fart, shit and turd have been established popular insults since the middle of the fifteenth century, the final extension of meaning has only taken place in the last two centuries for: bugger (1719), bastard (1830), fucker (1893), prick (1928), cunt (1929), tit (1947).

Bastard, as often as not nowadays a term of endearment, comes from the Old French for son of pack-saddle, somehow suggesting someone not born legitimately in bed. The French also used to talk of *coitrart*, son of a quilt, and the Germans of a *bankling*, son of a bench.

There is a continual sexual reference in most insults. Schmuck is Yiddish for foreskin, as well as being German for jewel. 'When they circumcised him, they threw away the wrong bit.' While the French are horrified to be called '*cochon*', and Germans '*schweinhund*', in England it is very insulting to call someone a 'cunt', even if the parts that ugly word denotes are the object of continuous speculation, fascination and veneration by most sentient males. Interestingly, 'fuck' in French is often rendered by the more gentle '*baiser*' which, of course, also means 'to kiss.'

Shakespeare provides a sumptuous hoard of sexual and non-sexual insults: 'roasted Manningtree ox with the pudding in his belly'; 'stuffed cloakbag of guts'; 'you whoreson peasant'; 'virgin-violator'; 'clod of wayward marl' (although Dunbar's 'cuntbitten crawdon' is competitive).

The arts and politics have produced some fine insults. On reading a bad review, according to his son and biographer Enrico Caruso Jnr., the great opera singer used to scream 'Imbecilli! Cretini! Bestie!' 'He is the sewer, not the sewage', John Biffen on Bernard Ingham. Gore Vidal said Truman Capote was a typist, not a writer. Jan Morris accused the greatly admired Bruce Chatwin of 'Snobbism, equally camp and genuine; showy connoisseurship of a quirky kind; the deadly energy of the raconteur; the insensitivity of the tuft-hunter.' James Rogers described Jeffrey Archer's literary style as a 'blend of bathos, egotism and wince-inducing crassness.' Cyril Connolly got Ernest Hemingway in one when he wrote of his 'sadistic facetiousness that went with a tendency to sentimentality.' Meanwhile, Philip Toynbee dismissed Connolly's 'hatred of England ... adulatory and snobbish love of France, embittered and boring connoisseurship of food and wine.'

There is a great deal in a name and surnames provide a starting point for an understanding of how we respect or disrespect others. Four great Roman families are named after beans: Fabius and *fava* have the same root. Surnames began as a means of classifying the masses in an age when tax collection began. In Italian it is as easy to stigmatise as to praise with a name. The suffix -*accio* is almost always pejorative. The quattrocento Florentine painter known as Masaccio would have a reputation ever so slightly tarnished if he were known as 'Skulking Tom.' On the other hand, Michelangelo Buonarroti seems to have been well starred if not from inception, at least from birth. Buonarroti (from *buon* 'good' and *arrota* 'gain') is a testament to his parents' gratitude at his birth. In his *I Cognomi Italiani* (1981) Emidio de Felice says Esposito ('exposed') is the most familiar surname in Naples. Some of de Felice's research is funded by an Italian telephone company: his exhaustive search through phone books has also revealed that the most popular Calabrian surname is Rotondo ('rotund'). Anybody called Quaglia ('quail') acquired his name because at some time in the past his ancestors were thought to be either timid, lecherous or fat, like the little game bird.

There is also the question of body languages. The New Zealand Maoris have their tradition of '*whakapohane*', exhibiting their buttocks. First noted by Captain Cook, the Queen has recently enjoyed this spectacle. The famous two-finger sign derives from the arrogant gesture made by the English archers at Agincourt. Demonstrating the second and third fingers was a gesture of defiance mingled with threat: the very essence of the insult.

IRONY

Irony is the glory of slaves. This is why the American master race is so very bad at it.

ITALIAN FOOD

Italians may have a reputation for art and learning—even though Erasmus, for example, only mentions one work by an Italian author—but for most people, Italy means food. It was Italians who taught the French about food.

In the history of cooking it was Italy which in the sixteenth century first emerged from the medieval soup of spices and sauces to offer dishes which are recognisably modern. Typical, according to Bartolomeo Scappi in his 1570 book about Pope Pius V's favourite recipes, were: prosciutto cooked in wine or spit roast partridges served with sliced lemon. The style is close to the best new wave Italian cooking, but it took considerable creative and promotional efforts to rescue Italian *cucina* from the morass of tomatoes and tinned sardines in which it has languished for most of the century. In his minor classic, *The Gourmet's Guide to Europe* (1903), Newnham Davis describes Italian cooking with the patrician fascination and tolerance of an Edwardian imperialist descending into the jungle:

There is no cookery in Europe so often maligned without cause as that of Italy.

And went on:

If you have any fear of the cook being too liberal with the best of all digestives you have only to say *senz' aglio* …

Somewhat condescendingly he accepted that,

An Italian cook fries better than one of any other nationality.

But amazingly believed that,

The fish of the Mediterranean are coarse and poor, compared with the glories of the Channel.

Newnham Davis' amused tolerance was not shared by Norman Douglas, author of the influential *Venus in the Kitchen*, and one of the main esoteric sources for Elizabeth David's post-War revival of Mediterranean cooking. Throughout his books *Siren Land* and *Old Calabria*, Douglas declares his hilarious revulsion with peasant customs and cooking.

Our understanding of the realities of Italian cooking has been complicated by patterns of immigration: most of the Italian emigrants to the United States and Britain came from the tomato-rich poor south, rather than the more patrician north. Newnham Davis described Milan as 'the town of white marble and veal cutlets'; that few emigrants came from the town of white risotto has distorted our picture of Italian cooking.

The revolution in Italian cooking is no less than the reinvention of an anthology of national stereotypes which turned the cornetto and tomato culture on its head. About twenty years ago the popular perception of Italy began to change. Somebody—probably in California—discovered that pasta was nutritious rather than fattening. Italy became a holiday destination for influential consumers and the entire image of the country was refreshed and modernised abroad by the international success of sophisticates such as Fausto Santini and Giorgio Armani. It is no coincidence that at just the time people started publishing books about renovating Tuscan farmhouses into conditions which reflected a taste for the blameless life of the *'contadino'*, while not foregoing the northern conveniences of kitchen gods called Neff, Bosch and AEG, or the small pleasures of a Dulux palette applied to a pigsty on the slopes of Radicofani or Castiglioncel del Trinoro, people also began to look for authentic Italian food.

They found it in Marcella Hazan. Her *Classic Italian Cooking* (1973) became immensely popular in both the United States and Britain, an inspiration to countless new restaurants, and was perhaps the single greatest influence in re-establishing the simple verities of Italian cooking; in Britain, of all places, Antonio Carluccio introduced a television audience to mushroom-hunting and in 1987, Anna del Conte published the encyclopaedic and magnificent *The Gastronomy of Italy*, a book whose scholarly content and authentic recipes made it an authoritative foundation for all subsequent accounts of Italian cooking.

Italy caters better than any European culture to our nostalgia for the mud. Here is simple food for sophisticated people: future sociologists will be fascinated at the way the most sophisticated Anglo-Saxon societies have been engineering the assumption of a world of peasant values, something which the 'revival' of Italian cooking so readily offers. At its best, the new wave is a rediscovery of the old values lost when restaurateurs could get by with cynicism, posters of Sorrento and a close relationship with an avocado supplier. Curiously, this new style of Italian cooking is almost unknown in Italy itself.

JAPANESE

The Japanese are very different from you and me. Deliberately so, on many counts. Inscrutability was Made in Japan. And so was scrutability: there is a form of Japanese striptease where the woman stands stationary and is examined by men holding magnifying glasses. They claim their language is impossible for foreigners to learn, but linguists say it is not all that difficult to speak. Writing may present special problems, but a basic conversation in Japanese is not beyond the means of someone who can manage one in Portuguese or Greek.

An ability to do well speaking Japanese may depend on having a creative imagination. If you have an inventive turn of mind, things may be easier: Walkman is only the most famous of the gloriously awful Japanese coinages in fractured, made-good but step-ahead English. Less well known, but equally winning, is their expression for topless (as in beaches or bars). This wonderful neologism is 'nopanty.'

Again, some Japanese believe, against all the most persuasive historical and technical evidence, that the gestation period for their children is ten months, as distinct to the Euro-American-normal nine. Some jaded *gaijin* insiders regard this as possible evidence that the Japanese have, in fact, come from outer space, since so much of their behaviour is contrary to what the rest of us regard as human nature, but the more rational explanation is that the Japanese wish to be seen as biologically different, as separate and as culturally superior as they are geographically insular. It would be wrong to call the Japanese a nation of racists, but they do have a keen sense of national identity.

Never mind that their art and philosophy and religion were so contumaciously stolen from China and Korea, that German technicians installed Tokyo's pressurised sanitation system, that even their celebrated late industrial deity of 'quality control' was introduced to them in the fifties by a group of American engineers, including W. Edwards Deming, Joseph Juran and Armand Feigenbaum, never mind that the most successful Japanese cars of recent years have been designed in America by Americans, the Japanese insist on their uniqueness. And here, of course, is a paradox of world historical dimensions. While they are busy remorselessly dominating world markets and equally busy consuming established European brands—thereby assuming status by a process similar to sympathetic magic—they want to remain inaccessible and remote. While they are eager to disport themselves at home or abroad in Western trinkets, beads and mirrors, whether from Ralph Lauren, Hermès, Dunhill or Gucci, their fundamental taste for exclusion means that every now and then the specifications for lenses of stoplights on foreign cars is changed so as to involve importers in intolerable expense and frustration.

Japan is a country of attitudes. The culture may entertain a great sense of beauty, but it has no sense of ugliness. If you were expecting Tokyo to be beguilingly oriental, you will be shocked at its trashy mid-Western hideousness. Appearances, behind the bamboo curtain, are at best deceptive, more likely confusing. Years after the occupying American forces told them it would be a good idea to give streets names, most taxi drivers are lost outside their own district. The visitor simply doesn't have a chance, unless his host draws him a map.

For every marvellously minimalist *riyokan* with its ethereal paper walls subtly dividing space with the elusive precision of a haiku, there is an absolutely disgusting lacquered Edwardian cabinet. For every austere tea ceremony there is baroque, noisy, vulgar and interminable *kabuki*. For every Buddhist rock garden there is a corruscatingly garish *pachinko* parlour full of terrifying low-life specimens with tattoos, flick-knives and some very antisocial habits. It is Western wish-fulfilment of Madame Butterfly sophistication to imagine Japan as a culture of cool, dignified restraint. When Aldous Huxley saw the Cherry Dances at Kyoto he said they were 'extraordinarily vulgar and garish.'

Our Western view of Japan is partial and specific. We have interpreted Japan through the eyes of observers who saw only what they wanted to see. They were conditioned in their perceptions by prevailing Western tastes, not by their real experiences, and the same is true today. There are many awesome things about modern Tokyo, but there are many awful things as well. Japan is not perfect: 35 per cent of roads are unpaved; less than 50 per cent of the population has mains drainage; only 40 per cent of the population even has *access* to a flushing lavatory and 80 per cent of Tokyo's electrical cables are overground. All that and for every 4.7 meter of paved or unpaved road you will find a motor car. Visitors are frequently dismayed by the suffocating smell of old fish and, as they are jostled by citizens whose culture teaches them to regard interior space as more valuable than external area, wonder wistfully about how these people ever acquired a reputation for ruthless organisation.

Future cultural historians will marvel at the curiously elegant fit between Japanese religion (with its dedication to detail, miniaturisation, discipline, ritual, routine, definition) and the imperatives of engineering for manufacture. Toyota has a test track with a long stretch of perfectly surfaced road: it is utterly flat except that near the centre it rises by just a few millimetres to compensate for the curvature of the earth.

JEWS

Twenty per cent of Jews appear to have a genetic mutation

which causes a disagreeable abreaction to alcohol. The mutation increases the level of acetaldehyde, the toxin which gives hangovers their characteristic features. Thus Israel has one of the lowest levels of alcholism in the developed world.

The Holocaust produced such unspeakable horrors that all polite opinions about Jews have to be made from a defensive and apologetic posture. This inhibits discussion about this remarkable people who have, to be absolutely fair to them, as many nebbishes, schlemiels, schmucks and schmoozers as any other readily identifiable ethno-religious caste. In fact there is no good definition of a Jew. Jonathan Miller once said he wasn't a Jew, he was Jewish. Very little other than a collective noun binds together, say, an irreligious Upper East Side billionaire and a shoeless nomadic Ethiopian ... except that both have a claim to be Jews.

The word Jew comes from the Hebrew Yehuda or Judah, the son of Jacob whose descendants made up one of the tribes of Israel.

The United States is the de facto home of the Jews. Israel is merely a theory. Jewish immigrants to colonial America were Sephardic (from the Hebrew *Sepharadhi*, Spain), driven out by the Inquisition. The very first to arrive was a group of twenty-three Jews of Dutch extraction who landed in New Amsterdam in 1654. The next great wave of immigration was the 200,000 or so German Jews (an expression first used in 1865). These educated middle-class Jews settled in the Mid-West between 1840 and 1860. Then more than three million Central European Jews arrived in the United States between 1880 and 1910. Speaking Yiddish, they experienced at first hand the dark literary fantasy which Franz Kafka described in *Amerika*. These were Ashkenazi Jews, from the Hebrew for the Biblical Armenia. Of course, they came from elsewhere as well, but this was a suitably exotic description for dark, primitive, superstitious people from the shtetls (a diminutive of *Stadt* —

town) and it has endured. They settled in Manhattan's Lower East Side where they established sweatshops.

These Jews soon began to attract a rich vocabulary of derogatory terms for which English provided many precedents. By the early seventeenth century, 'Jew' already meant a crafty trader, a concept made famous by Shakespeare. The nineteenth century gave us 'Hebe' (from Hebrew) and 'Kike' (because illiterate Jews landing at Ellis Island refused to sign with a suspiciously Christian-looking cross and used a circle — *kikel* — instead). 'Yid' comes from the German '*Jude.*'

But the literary waves travelled the other way as well. Yiddish — a coarse but evocative language — made a rich contribution to American English. Particularly words beginning with schm (schmeer, schmooze, schmuck), now often invented and used to convey irony. Bagel. Chutzpah. Dreck (crap). Ish kabible — That should be my biggest problem — a cult expression of 1910. Kibitz (from the German '*Kiebitz*' or lapwing, something that flutters around). We have mazuma for money and meshuganeh for a stupid person, mensch for one of the boys. A nebbish is an ineffectual person, a schlemiel an unlucky, gullible or credulous one. We all, from time to time, schlepp. Schlock is from German *Schlag*, a blow, and suggests broken, therefore devalued, merchandise.

The Jews have a reputation for stinginess reinforced by profound cultural convictions. Throughout the last part of his life Isaac Bashevis Singer dined three times a week at The Famous Dairy Restaurant on Broadway and West 72nd Street. One day Mr Orenstein, the owner, asked him why he never, ever left a tip. His reply: 'My heart won't allow it.'

KISSING

'The kiss' according to F. Scott Fitzgerald in *The Crack-Up* (1945), 'originated when the first male reptile licked the first female reptile, implying in a subtle, complimentary way that she was as succulent as the small reptile he had for dinner the night before.' This is not quite so fanciful as it sounds. Entomologists believe that the interaction of antennae during the sexual intercourse of snails and insects is in its nature a sort of kiss. Certainly, the kiss (from Old English *cyssan*, 'to press or touch with the lips, in token of affection, greeting, or reverence'), seems to be common to all mammals, but not to the Japanese. According to the exotic Lafcadio Hearn in *Out of the East* (1895), 'Kisses and embraces are simply unknown in Japan as tokens of affection.' In Rome the kiss was more a sign of reverence and respect than a means of sexual excitation.

In some parts of the world, the olfactory kiss is far more common than the tactile kiss. Lapps and Yakuts like to sniff each other rather than put their tongues in each other's mouths. Swahili boys are taught to raise their loincloths as a salutation to women visitors who customarily smell their penises. The Chinese traditionally regard the European kiss as disgustingly suggestive of cannibalism. Indeed, even in some European cultures there is a sadistic element to kissing: in *Penthesilea* Heinrich Kleist's heroine remarks that (in German) the word for kiss (*Küße*) rhymes with bite (*Bisse*) and adds solemnly that when you are in love the 'heart may easily confound the two.' Japan's repudiated minority, the 'hairy' Ainu, much prefer biting to kissing. In his esoteric study, *Alone with the Hairy Ainu* (1893), A.H. Savage Landor reports an episode with a hairy Ainu girl who started nibbling his little finger and got herself so worked-up in a sequential process that she ended up biting his cheeks and all parts in between.

Kissing is culturally specific: Tamils prefer to rub noses rather than kiss during sexual intercourse and kissing of any kind is unknown among the North-American Indians. So where did the contemporary erotic kiss—also known as tongue sushi, a preppy expression for French kissing—come from? According to Compayre in his *L'Evolution intellectuelle et morale de l'enfant* (1893), the origin of the kiss is in the child's attraction to the maternal nipple: a basic association of well-being is extended to any desired object which is then sucked or licked. The modern erotic kiss is a sign of high refinement and is only practised in civilisations where the cultivation of pleasure is considered a proper cultural pursuit. In *The Perfumed Garden,* it is said that a 'moist kiss is better than a hasty coitus.' It is the relationship between the erotic kiss and a high state of civilisation that makes the tepid English talk about the French kiss. Mistinguett, 'Queen of the Paris Music Hall', explained its subtlety in an interview with *Theatre Review* in December 1955: 'A kiss can be a comma, a question mark or an exclamation point. That's basic spelling that every woman ought to know.'

KITSCH

Kitsch is the corpse that's left behind when anger leaves art ...

The term 'kitsch' — meaning bad art — comes from the German expression *'etwas Verkitschen'* which means, approximately, to knock something off. As Umberto Eco says, the meaning is so precise that it is unnecessary even to attempt a translation. Examples of kitsch include maudlin funerary monuments at, say, Forest Lawn or Père Lachaise, films and paintings with exaggerated emotional content and any form of interior decoration not sanctioned by tradition. To sophisticates kitsch is repulsive, but ever since the publication of Gillo Dorfles' *Kitsch* in 1969 (which defined the genre), a knowing group of pseudo-intellectuals have celebrated it in a too-clever-by-half way. Kitsch, whatever the medium, can easily be detected. There are two tests. Anything which lacks any reaction other than shock or popularity is kitsch. It is easily digestible pseudo-art for lazy people.

Context plays a fundamental role in our perception of kitsch. There are to be found in any object, image or gesture that is kitsch the following: a lack of proportion, an inappropriateness and a lack of tact. It is not always the object or gesture that is in itself kitsch, as the *intention*. In his book *Deutscher Kitsch* (1962) Walter Killy produced a pastiche of pulp fiction mixed up with passages from Rainer Maria Rilke. In the lowbrow context, the highbrow author was unrecognisable.

LEATHER

Leather is animal skin prepared for use by tanning. The word has been known since the Middle English period. Nowadays it has acquired salacious associations, pertaining, at best, to both heterosexual and homosexual sensualists and, at worst, sadists and masochists. In the United States, the wearing of a particular style of leather jacket is an explicit declaration that you favour sado-masochistic practices. Those who are 'into leather' will seek establishments where 'discipline' is available. They will also enjoy what is coyly known as 'rough stuff', a catalogue of violent or unhygienic practices involving: rubber (which means giving or taking a beating with a garden hose), water sports (urine showers or colonic enemas), TV training (role playing in transvestite costumes), diapering (using nappies), suspension hoists (experiments with pulleys and ropes and chains), infibulation (piercing of nipples or genitalia) or straightforward wrestling.

The association of tanned animal hide with these curious practices may have its source in the same animus that gives rise to shoe-fetishism, a minor perversion that has a number of significant literary sources of which the most attractive is the *oeuvre* of Restif de la Bretonne (1734-1806). In all other respects normal, except insofar as he was a talented writer, Restif found shoes a useful and eventually necessary adjunct to masturbation. His first literary success was *Le Pied de Fanchette* (1769), about a girl blessed with charming feet. Later, his affair with Charlotte Parangon (the wife of his employer) involved him using her shoes as a receptacle for his lust when her loins were not available. According to Richard von Krafft-Ebbing in *Psychopathia Sexualis*, scientific research at the turn of the century indicated that the smell of leather caused a direct sexual response in a significant number of men and women.

LIFE

Lived forwards, but understood backwards. According to Thomas Hobbes, 'solitary, poor, nasty, brutish and short.'

LUXURY

Santayana on luxury:

Having lived a peaceful, independent life, free from hardship or misfortune, I have found it easy to conform externally with the mechanism of society. Matter has been kind to me, and I am a lover of matter. Not only aesthetically but dynamically, as felt by Lucretius, nature to me is a welcome presence; and modern progress in mechanical invention and industrial luxury has excited joyously my materialistic imagination.

The rot set into the meaning of luxury in Britain when some time in the nineteen fifties a hotshot marketeer working for Ford decided that a premium priced model of the Ford Anglia might be ennobled with the name 'de luxe.' In the poetics of car specifications, de luxe here meant the addition of external chrome strips, elaborated mouldings around the rear light clusters and two-tone upholstery. It was hard for words to recover from such debasement so that nowadays in Britain 'luxury' is haphazardly applied to, say, a motor coach or a kitchen which are just plain ordinary.

In America, where the achievement of status has long been measured in terms of accumulated possessions, the idea of luxury has acquired a fetishistic quality. It can be defined by a powerful and evocative laundry list of artefacts. In her autobiography, the actress Ali McGraw describes her astonishment on arrival in Hollywood. The house was mock Georgian on a huge plot, with an intravenously fed three-hundred-year-old sycamore. There were scented candles (a sure definition of luxury at work) and in the linen cabinets hundreds of bars of Guerlain's 'Fleur des Alpes' soap.

Although Flaubert posed as the 'homme serieux' and defined luxury as 'the ruin of nations', the French are more confident with their tastes and senses than the English or the Americans. There is something marvellous about French culture which allows intellectual rigour to go hand in hand with intense sensual delight. One explanation of this may be psychological. Paris psychiatrist Michel Lejoyeux says he has identified a form of obsessive-compulsive disorder which seeks gratification from buying things, as if the act of purchasing (irrespective of eventual use) establishes power and authority over a harrowing world. Anthony Storr held a similar belief: while it is true that people feel rich when they are happy and experience financial anxiety when they are sad (irrespective of their actual worth), reckless expense may to certain neurotics be seen as a way of integrating themselves with the life force, a sort of Jungian buy-me/be-me adventure. Quite unconsciously, the extravagant and largely redundant baubles so expertly marketed by luxury businesses cater to this need.

MADNESS

'The great proof of madness', according to one of Napoleon's maxims, 'is the disproportion of one's designs to one's means.' Jung said 'show me a sane man and I will cure him for you.'

There are two ways to go mad: one, to think of too many things at the same time; two, to think of one thing to the exclusion of all else.

But it is notoriously difficult to define madness in any satisfactory way. To say so is not a modish reluctance to victimise the unfortunate, but a simple matter of observation. Mad people are *different*, they behave differently, unpredictably or oddly, but their differences are characterful and various. This was a familiar idea as long ago as the beginning of the seventeenth century. In his *Anatomy of Melancholy* (1621) Robert Burton says there are as many kinds of madness as there are madmen.

The only sensible definition of madness is that it defines itself. To many doctors a test for madness is the extent to which the sufferer acknowledges his oddness. Apparently, to a statistically significant degree, people who appear barking mad often regard themselves as entirely sane. To mutter 'Oh God, I think I'm going mad' is rather healthy, if tiresome.

The case of Phineas Gage shows that physical damage to the brain can cause fundamental changes in behaviour. In 1848, Gage, a foreman on the New England Railroad, had an accident with an explosive device causing a huge iron tamping rod to enter his eye and go crashing through his brain, exiting his skull and taking a significant portion on the frontal lobes with it. He was quite alright, except that he lost the ability to make ethical decisions. Ever since, there has been continuous debate about whether madness is caused by mechanical, chemical, or social defects. A modern account of a similar phenomenon occurs in Peter Matthiessen's haunting story 'Midnight Turning Grey' (1984).

Equally, brain chemistry influences behaviour. We get the expression 'mad as a hatter', an expression current in the United States in the thirties, known to Thackeray, but popularised by Lewis Carroll in *Alice in Wonderland* (1865), from an old health and safety at work issue involving a chemical called mercurous nitrate, held to be essential in the manufacture of felt hats. Deadly poisonous, it can produce a range of symptoms beginning with mild tremor and culminating in St Vitus Dance, a condition where all rational control of the body's motor functions are lost to unelected, unrequired and unexpected spasms. Today, alterations to brain chemistry are treatments for depression, a disorder on the lower slopes of madness. The popular drug Prozac is in the so-called SSRI (selective serotonin re-uptake inhibitor) class, working to control the level of serotonin and noradrenaline, important neuro-transmitters.

Consistently in the literature of madness, the idea of differentness dominates all descriptions of the state. The Spanish philosopher Gracian (1601-1658) said 'Better mad with the rest of the world than wise alone', an idea which resurfaces in Diderot's *Supplement au Voyage Bougainville* (1796) when he writes 'There is less harm to be suffered in being mad among madmen than in being sane all by oneself.' In the idea of collectiveness and separation we have the germ of the recently fashionable theory that madness can be defined statistically, although in the seventeenth century the playwright Nathaniel Lee, writing from Bedlam, said 'They called me mad, and I called them mad, and damn them, they outvoted me.' The statistical definition of madness means, crudely, that if more than half the given group perform in a certain way, then that defines normality and to depart from it is a sign of madness. This interpretation of madness found its extreme form in the perversions of medical ethics current in the darkest days of the Soviet Union when wheedling psychiatrists would routinely diagnose as madness any form of political dissent.

At about the same time R.D. Laing in Britain and Thomas Szasz in America declared that madness was an oppressive construct, an invention of the medical profession, a claim difficult to justify in the case of a straitjacketed lunatic sitting slobbering in a pool of his own excrement and, incidentally, also one which Dr Laing's and Dr Szasz' subsequent (and rather odd) personal histories tended to undermine.

Samuel Beckett's *Waiting for Godot* (1952) contains the line

'We are all born mad. Some remain so.'

MANNERS

Voltaire said that to succeed in the world it is not only necessary to be well mannered, you have to be stupid as well. The word 'etiquette' was coined by Lord Chesterfield, evidence that we associate the development of manners with French civilisation. The French distinction between the (intimate) second person singular and the (formal) second person singular allows real scope for well-mannered rebuffs illustrative of the social gradations on which manners depend. An aide opportunistically asked the dying de Gaulle *'Monsieur Le President, pourrai-je tu-toyer?'* De Gaulle replied *'Oui. Si vous voulez.'*

In his magisterial work, *The Civilizing Process* (1939), Norbert Elias explains that internalising emotions is a major part of the process of civilisation. Meanwhile, back to Lord Chesterfield, who encouraged his son to 'make love to every handsome woman you meet, and be gallant with all the rest.'

It was said of Stafford Cripps that he believed the sign of a gentleman was deliberately to compliment the plainest woman in a room. Meanwhile, in our own day, it is said that Lord (Jacob) Rothschild makes his driver get out of the car before he begins a row with his wife. Goethe knew that manners reside in a moral principle—that of making other people feel comfortable.

It is more than a generation since the publication of Alan Ross and Nancy Mitford's *U and Non-U Revisted* and we have acquired a whole new species of keywords. 'Serviette' may still cause 'shudders'? Lord Chesterfield again: 'The vulgar often laugh, but never smile; whereas well-bred people often smile, but seldom laugh. A witty thing never excited laughter; it pleases only the mind, and never distorts the countenance.' On the other, more positive, hand, Beaumarchais, author of *The*

Marriage of Figaro, said '*Je me presse de rire de tout de peur d'être obligé d'en pleurer*—I'll laugh about anything for fear I might have to weep.'

MISTRESS

James Goldsmith, the British financier and polygamist, warned that 'when you marry your mistress, you create a vacancy', but serial marriage has generally replaced the mistress for men under fifty. Yet the idea of this quaint institution fascinates.

A mistress was a woman kept in a service flat which would be spruce and trim. Maybe she was a poor divorcee or a widow who needed to provide for school fees. She was kept for sex which most likely occurred in what Tom Driberg called that awkward gap between tea and evensong. The French call it '*la cinq-à-sept.*' She was not a prostitute and would be faithful. She would be heterosexual. Inevitably she was not the social equivalent of her keeper and would never be seen out with him. She was something like the Roman concubine, or the French *femme d'attente*, shop girls or minor tradeswomen who eked out a living by providing a foretaste of marriage to students, or an illusion of it to those too poor to afford it.

The mistress offered a powerfully aphrodisiac transgression of taboo, yet, curiously the relationship she enjoyed and the environment she occupied were closely modelled on the conventional bourgeois matrimonial establishment, but without the bureaucratic rituals of marriage or the spiritual comforts of love. The mistress was an invention of the first age of mass-consumption when, suddenly, everything was for sale (at a price). Mistresses were a product of the division of labour, an opportunistic creation of the same urban, industrial society that gave us the department store and railway timetables and every other hierarchical, bureaucratised institution. The nineteenth-century creation of the mistress was one reaction to the schizophrenia which urban industrial cultures imposed on women: mother? companion? lover? whore? The mistress offered a solution: separation of love and sex, of man and animal (which the business of marriage so artfully combines), all contained within comfortingly bourgeois rituals and rendez-vous. She takes her place in the history of venal sex, alongside the 'common' prostitute. To understand this we have to look to France where the landscape of the libido sits in clearer air than in England.

Significantly, there are no written accounts from nineteenth-century French prostitutes to explain their views of their calling or their predicament. We have to rely on Zola, Toulouse-Lautrec, Huysmans and Flaubert, to sketch the landscape of *galanterie* which describes the lives of the victims and beneficiaries of the agonies of male desire. These intense descriptions and images have given us an intense, but misleadingly specific, vision. The *grande horizontale*, described by Zola in *Nana,* was a splendid creature who might live in a majestic apartment, spend all day at her *toilette*, drive in the Bois du Boulogne, attend first nights or private views and 'entertain' at home over, or under, a late dinner.

The *maison de passe* was an unlicensed brothel of the lowest class which, as its name suggests, was neither directed nor decorated with a view to long-term pleasure, more nearly to provide opportunities to have spasms of the groin in exchange for money: 'Are you going to make me rich?' was the familiar come-on of Parisian streetwalkers. More elaborate was the *maison de tolerance*, the type of brothel which strove for elaborate effects designed to impress the lower-middle classes. It is the *maison de tolerance* that provides us with the plush velour notion of the brothel: here Apollinaire's Prince Mony Vibescu took his considerable pleasures, as described in his extraordinarily salacious book, *Les Onze milles verges* (a play on words: 'verge' is vernacular for penis and very nearly *vierge*, or virgin).

Lastly, and more nearly approaching the middle-class institution of the mistress, was the *maison de rendez-vous*, the locale for the type of venal sex preferred by a social elite. Here drink was not served and if they did not actually have the manners themselves, the women aped the manners and appearances of the bourgeois marriage. Just as mistresses were always kept in Kensington service flats, or just possibly in a semi in Barnes, you would find a *maison de rendez-vous* located in the fashionable areas close to the new department stores, the idea being that middle-class women in search of cash or adventure could visit them without too much notice. Money only changed hands via a third party, not between client and provider. In a *maison de rendez-vous* what you expected to find was another man's wife.

MODERNISM

Modernism is the belief, still current, that the twentieth century had unique, precious and original perceptions of the world which should replace all predecessors which are then condemned to history. Modernists are enemies of traditions and heritage, except their own. The celebrated French interior designer Andrée Putman, a pupil of the composer François Poulenc, said 'modernity does not deny earlier forms ... it does deny traditions.' 'Modern' is a well established description of art, literature and architecture, but in fact first became current in the Church to describe the refreshing attitude which re-examined the Bible and doctrine in the light of contemporary philosophy and technological innovation. Modern thought was roundly condemned by Pope Pius X in 1907 in his encyclical *Pascendi*, where he stigmatised it as the 'synthesis of all heresies', a description of which its proponents would be proud.

Rimbaud's *'Il faut être absolument moderne'* defined the mood and so did T.S. Eliot's 1917 description of a 'modern girl' which in both cases meant someone who wanted to smoke, drink, dance and very possibly fornicate liberally, prosecuting irreligious beliefs the while. For many Modernists the implied act of rebellion was the real sport and as soon as, circa 1970, it became the orthodoxy its creative force was spent. Modernism means, among many other things, a collective and highly self-conscious sense of aesthetic purpose. Only with battles to be fought and won was it an interesting crusade.

Considerable debate surrounds the origins of post-modernism, a term coined by Arnold Toynbee in 1938 to describe the new cycle of history which, in his interpretation, began in 1875. As much effort is involved in defining it. In architecture or literature (the two areas where the modernist ethic was strongest) post-modernism means a rejection of the moral certainties of its predecessor. In architectural theory the influential apologists of modernism based their arguments on a compelling mixture of Darwin's and Marx's methodologies. The idea was that modernism was the end of a journey, an inevitable result of what had gone before. This was what the historian Herbert Butterfield called *The Whig Interpretation of History* (1931). Ironically, for a subject which was so influenced by the romance of machinery, it was technology that undermined modernist theory. The old verities of 'truth to materials' and form having some relationship with function are, paradoxically, Victorian ideas which could not sustain their own viability in a more complicated age.

In literature and literary theory, modernism was defined by Ford Madox Ford in the Preface to his *Collected Poems* (1913) when he said his artistic purposes were 'to register my own times in terms of my own time.' Post-modernism is now the established term for that sensibility that rejects the idea that Modernism is the supreme and universal expression of the contemporary spirit. Post-modernism has been most influential in architecture where its presence can be identified by gaudy colours, facetious decoration, irrational shapes which confer on buildings the ability to become tiresome very quickly. Modern architecture, however, has now become an all but meaningless notion. Lacking the purpose and moral direction of the thirties, it also lacks emotion and wider meaning, indulging too often in gratuitous shape-making. Modern buildings tend to be architectural one-liners.

MONDEGREEN

A mondegreen is an example of paronomasia, a comically misheard phrase. Its source is a misconstruction of the Scottish folksong whose refrain went,

> They ha' slain the Duke of Erroll
> And laid him on the green.

The last few words were construed as 'Lady Mondegreen.' Another example is that mis-hearing of Edith Piaf's haunting lament 'L'Avion Rose.' Mondegreens were championed by the American humorist Sylvia Wright (1917-1981) who describes them in her book *Get Away from Me with Those Christmas Presents*.

MOUNTAINS

Mountains are, naturally, the cause of mountaineering. This odd sport is characteristic of the heroic perverseness of human inspiration. 'The essence of mountaineering as a sport' says Arnold Lunn, an Alpinist and commercial exploiter of skiing, 'is the solution of the problems which the mountain provides.' This is hilariously near the commonplace about mountains.

The commonplace about mountains is that people climb them because they are *there*. But for most of European history the majority has rather wished they were not. One evening, according to Lord Balfour of Inchrye, Churchill was in the smoking room of the House of Commons when shown an article in the evening paper on the Mount Everest conquest. His opinion was: 'I do not wish to overrate chastity, but there is much to be said for virgin mountains.'

Mountains are a fixed point in the evolving catalogue of contemporary values. The conventional response is almost always one of benign awe. Certainly, mountains provide magnificent stuff for metaphors. And the most famous one of the mountain in labour is an ancient one. A mighty effort made for a small effect. The allusion is to the celebrated line *'Parturient montes, nascetur ridiculus mus* — Mountains will be in labour and the birth will be a funny little mouse', by Horace (*Ars Poetica*, 139). A similar quotation occurs in Aesop.

Judaeo-Christianity with its central belief in a beneficent God disposed western man to admire mountains: they were symbols of God's awesome creative power. But classical civilisation had neither awe, nor respect nor even interest in mountains or mountain scenery. The Greek gods were omnipresent. They were respected or feared, but they were not loved. The Romantic idea that nature is beautiful is a direct development of the Christian concept of an all-power divine creator who revealed himself through his creations. The Greeks, on the other hand, worried out an earthbound humanism that made them more susceptible to man-made art than to natural beauty. The Greeks detested *apeiron*, things without limits.

Mankind's affair with mountains began with Petrarch who climbed Mount Ventoux in Provence on 26th April, 1335, and became the first writer to describe a mountain in favourable terms. (To Dante mountains were simply opportunities to hang a few well-worn Homeric epithets. Mountains were 'hard' or 'bad' or 'broken.' The same attitude can be seen in the work of Early Renaissance painters: before the eighteenth century no mountain was painted accurately from life.) But mountains were still regarded as horrible. Perhaps the first expression of delight in mountains was a diary entry of John Evelyn's in 1644 while on the Grand Tour: he has an ecstatic revelation and his initial horror is translated into a sense of wonder.

Bishop Berkely at Mont Cenis in the Alps in 1714 was 'much put out of humour by the most horrible precipices'. Later Samuel Johnson was still dismissing them as 'considerable protuberances.' Oliver Goldsmith said that the scenery in the Highlands would be fine except 'hills and rocks intercept every prospect.' In 1856 Ruskin said mountains were a source of 'happiness far fuller and more beneficent than all the bright fruitfulness of the plain'.

Reminiscing for the publication of Arnold Lunn's *Switzerland and the English* in 1944, founder members of The Alpine Club all agreed that they owed their love of mountains to the inspiration of Ruskin (elected to the club on the basis of *Modern Painters* where, in volume four, in 'Mountain Glory', he took up with all the magnificence at his disposal the argument that mountains are a source of perpetual beauty whose power is derived directly from God). They existed nor merely to purify and move air, soil and water but to 'fill the thirst of the human heart for the beauty of God's working.'

Love of mountains was inseparable from Ruskin's theocentric philosophy as when he argued that a cottage made of granite could never be wholly miserable. If mountains were 'natural cathedrals' then any dwelling made out of mountains necessarily shared the nobility and purity and divinity of nature. Perhaps thinking of Ruskin, Auden said the 'mountain-snob is a Wordsworthian fruit.'

NATIONAL IDENTITY

C.P. Snow was certainly right when he said the majority of what we call 'traditions' was an invention of the nineteenth century. Welsh national costume was, for instance, invented by Lady Llandovery. And the historian Hugh Trevor-Roper showed that the Highland kilt was, in fact, the invention of a

Quaker ironmaster in Lancashire in the 1780s.

NOVELS

What is a novel? G.K. Chesterton says 'A good novel tells us the truth about its hero; but a bad novel tells us the truth about its author.' To Robert Louis Stevenson 'Fiction is to the grown man what play is to the child; it is there that he changes the atmosphere and tenor of his life.' According to Thoreau 'A book should contain pure discoveries, glimpses of terra firma, though by shipwrecked mariners, and not the art of navigation by those who have never been out of sight of land.' According to Angus Wilson 'All fiction is for me a kind of magic and trickery — a confidence trick, trying to make people believe something is true that isn't.'

What is worth reading? The young Ernest Hemingway used to visit the rather older Gertrude Stein in her 27 rue de Fleurus apartment where she gave him *alcools* and literary advice. In his reminiscence of his Paris years, *A Moveable Feast* (1964), Hemingway says Stein told him that he should only ever read the truly good or the frankly bad. Emerson's comment is famous: 'People do not deserve to have good writing, they are so pleased with bad.' Great advice, but who's to determine quality? Philip Larkin had a perfect test for quality in a novel: 'Could I read it? If I could read it, did I believe it? If I believed it, did I care about it? And if I cared about it, what was the quality of my caring, and would it last?'

The techniques of writing a novel are fascinating. Popular novelists who create page-turners feed the reader a continuous diet of, on the one hand, curiosity and unease, and on the other, explanation and relief. E.M. Forster, in *Aspects of the Novel*, wrote 'what is fictitious in a novel is not so much the story but the method by which thought develops into action, a method which never occurs in daily life.'

The death of the novel has been pronounced in every

decade of this century. A great many readers, critics and even novelists themselves believe that film has overtaken the novel as a source of popular literary and artistic concern, although some hold out hope for The Great American Novel … although the greatest American novelist Don DeLillo has ambitions for The Global Novel, whatever that might be.

The crisis is illustrated by the long-running argument between the populist Tom Wolfe and the less popular American literary establishment.

In a masterpiece of literary snobbery, John Updike said *Bonfire of the Vanities* was 'entertainment, not literature.' Indicating what's wrong with literature, Tom Wolfe's reply was that writers like Updike, who rely on their imagination rather than close observation of life as it is really lived, have lost access to a vital critical technique. He insisted that, by 1969, magazine writers like himself had a technical edge over the best novelists. Furthermore, Wolfe argued, sales of his books rather supported his view.

In 1989 Wolfe published an essay in the rightish, intellectual US magazine *Harpers* called 'Stalking the Billion-Footed Beast.' He said the American novel was dying of anorexia, that he alone represented the true literary tradition of Juvenal, Swift, Addison and Steele. Not unsurprisingly, the anorexic novelists (Wolfe is very keen on figure metaphors and in *Bonfire* had given us 'social X-rays' to describe professionally thin women) took the bait. John Updike, Norman Mailer and John Irving, later insulted by Wolfe as 'The Three Stooges', made their claim for leadership in the contest for possession of The Great American Novel. It was a classic debate of high culture versus popular. It was a new version of George Santayana's dilemma about culture: if profound and noble it must remain rare, if common it must become mean.

John Irving said reading Wolfe was 'like reading a bad newspaper or a bad piece in a magazine. It makes you wince.'

Note here the suggestion that newspaper and magazine writing is *inevitably* inferior to 'literature.' Wolfe shot back 'insular, effete and irrelevant'; he called Mailer and Updike 'two piles of bones.' Irving, author of *The World According to Garp*, said that on any page of Wolfe he could find a sentence that would make him gag.

Then Norman Mailer joined in. He said reading Wolfe's *Man in Full* was like making love to a 300lb woman: 'Once she gets on top, it's all over. Fall in love or get asphyxiated.' 'It's the lead dog ... they always bite in the ass' Wolfe said, to which Mailer (rather amusingly) rejoined 'It doesn't mean you're the top dog because your ass is bleeding.'

NUDITY

Montaigne said 'Man is the sole animal whose nudities offend his own companions, and the only one who, in his natural actions, withdraws and hides himself from his own kind.' The word 'nude' meant bare or naked as early as the sixteenth century, it was not used as a euphemism for the naked condition of the human body until the nineteenth century except in reference to art.

We have a range of euphemisms to accommodate our anxieties about nudity. 'In the Altogether' has its source in George du Maurier's *Trilby* (1894, an influential book as it is also the source of the name for the hat). Here the artist's model says: 'I sit for the altogether.' A form of the word – 'Altogethery', which meant drunk – was used by Byron in a letter of 1816. Its connotation there (that a drunken man lounged about) may have influenced the later use of the term to denote the relaxed or lounging pose of a nude model. 'In the buff' is an American expression, euphemistically suggestive of tanned leather, and 'au naturel' is currently a popular nicety for nudity. Many Americans still find French more elegant and more evasive than English. A current American phrase for 'naked', this euphemism functions partially by substituting presumably elegant French for coarse English.

Any discussion of nudity brings into play the erogenous zones, of which the buttocks and the breasts are the most familiar. Studies of nineteenth-century photography, or at least of 'artistic' nudes, show that buttocks (what the dictionary defines as the protuberances of the rump) were the focus of erotic fascination for generations. Someone once said of those great nineteenth-century literary figures, Hilaire Belloc and G.K. Chesterton, that they were 'two buttocks of one bum', perhaps without the erotic tinge.

Nowadays the buttocks are the most innocent of the erogenous zones. There is a detailed definition in an ordinance on public nudity drafted by the commissioners of St John's County, Florida:

The area at the rear of the human body (sometimes referred to as the gluteus maximus) which lies between two imaginary straight lines running parallel to the ground when a person is standing, the first or top such line being a half inch below the top of the vertical cleavage of the nates (i.e. the prominence formed by the muscles running from the back of the hip to the back of the leg) and the second or bottom such line being a half-inch above the lowest point of the curvature of the fleshy protuberance (sometimes referred to as the gluteal fold), and between two imaginary straight lines, one on each side of the body (the 'outside lines'), which outside lines are perpendicular to the ground and to the horizontal lines described above, and which perpendicular outside lines pass through the outermost point(s) at which each nate meets the outer side of each leg. Notwithstanding the above, buttocks shall not include the leg, the hamstring muscle below the gluteal fold, the tensor faciae latae muscles, or any of the above described portion of the human body that is between either (i) the left inside perpendicular line and the left outside perpendicular line or (ii) the right inside perpendicular line and the right outside perpendicular line. For the purpose of the previous sentence, the left inside perpendicular line shall be an imaginary straight line on the left side of the anus (i) that is perpendicular to the ground and to the horizontal lines described above and (ii) that is one third of the distance from the anus to the left outside line. (The above description can *generally* be described as covering one third of the buttocks centred over the cleavage for the length of the cleavage.)

The female breasts are secondary sexual characteristics, but have a primary role in both genders' preoccupations with sex and style. Freud's account of the significance of the mammaries may be too abstruse, although there is doubtless substantial oedipal complexity in organs which simultaneously signal motherhood and, when revealed outside the context of lactation, suggest sexual availability. Psychologists believe that the link between motherhood and sexual gratification (to both parties) has its source in the sense of touch common to both breast-feeding and to fondling.

At the turn of the century, psychologists were busy determining the physiological and neural links between the breast and the primary sexual organs. Mad German scientists attached electrodes to the nipples of volunteers and measured the consequential contraction of the uterus to prove that the act of suckling produces in most women a voluptuous sexual response. The link between the tit and sexual gratification was explained by Havelock Ellis in his magisterial *Studies in the Psychology of Sex* (1897-1910):

As one of the chief secondary sexual characters in women, and one of her chief beauties, a woman's breasts offer themselves to the lover's lips with a less intimate attraction than her mouth only because the mouth is better able to respond. On her side, such contact is often instinctively desired. Just as the sexual disturbance of pregnancy is accompanied by a sympathetic disturbance in the breasts, so the sexual excitement produced by the lover's proximity reacts on the breasts; the nipple becomes turgid and erect in sympathy with the clitoris; the woman craves to place her lover in the place of the child, and experiences a sensation in which these two supreme objects of her desire are deliciously mingled.

The English language is full of vulgarisms and synonyms revealing the complex fascination of tits. An internal 1993 memorandum from Fox Television (reprinted in *Spy* magazine, February 1994) is a perfect exposition of the place of the tit in everyday life. The memo concerns a forthcoming programme about women with notably large breasts and the author is concerned with the station's 'Standards and Practices.' Fox Television said that while the words 'tits' and 'knockers' are *not* allowable, no exception would be made to the use of boobs, bazongas, jugs, hooters and snack trays.

OPERA

Schopenhauer detested opera — 'vapid drama and mock poetry.' 'Grand opera is not really a product of the pure artistic sense, it is rather the somewhat barbaric conception of enhancing aesthetic enjoyment by piling up the means to it' (*Aesthetics*). Somewhere between here and Andre Previn's definition of 'fat broads yowling' lies the essential truth.

Schopenhauer had a purist view of music, which he regarded — especially in the forms of the mass and the symphony — as the highest of the arts. To distract from its essential and abstract force by programmatic reference or dramatic context was, in his view, a travesty. Music required 'the undivided and undistracted attention of the entire mind.'

Opera lets the eye invade the mind, polluting the pleasure to be taken from the 'sacred, mysterious, intimate language of music.'

Opera deadens our musical receptivity through its three hours duration and tests our patience by lethargic dramatic development through what is usually a very trite action. It is in itself intrinsically and essentially boring. In 1806, the sentimentalist writer and playwright August von Kotzebue (1761-1819) described Beethoven's *Fidelio* as 'incoherent, shrill, chaotic and ear-splitting.'

OPINIONS

The Duke of Wellington disapproved of his soldiers cheering as this was too nearly an expression of opinion (a privilege which he would deny the rabble).

Opinions are one example of an informed pattern of thought, although the contemptuous character of the familiar remark 'that's a matter of opinion' shows that opinions are not always respectable. To change an opinion without a mental process is a mark of the uneducated.

Opinions are in a hierarchy which begins with axioms. Axioms are self-evident truths. Next come epigrams, short witty sayings which are valid in only one particular case and have no general relevance. Aphorisms are short, clever statements, usually of a literary character, which may be said to contain a general truth, but since they concern style and manners rather than science, they are not susceptible to strict quantification. Aphorisms tend to be longer than epigrams and are what Auden described as 'aristocratic' in character since 'the successful aphorist never feels under any compunction to explain or justify his position and, equally, is convinced of the superiority of his own point of view to that of his readers.'

But it is a small step from the bright, successful aphorism to the ordinary truism and from the truism to the dull platitude.

Opinions are more free and interesting. As Samuel Johnson said of wit, opinions should be both natural and new. The tepid waters of platitude can be avoided with a cargo of cynicism. The skilled opinion former has something of the aphorist's disdain for the intellect of his audience, but is—by nature of the conversational context which is normally the accommodation of an opinion—more likely to tolerate discussion of, even disagreement about, his pronouncements.

So, an opinion is a lengthy aphorism with a point of view. Aphorisms date from the early history of medicine when the evolution of scientific knowledge in this field was empirical, spasmodic and cumulative. Short, sharp definitions and observations were the most efficient way of recording the progress of knowledge. The word was first found in the *Aphorisms of Hippocrates*, spiritual father of modern medicine, which begins with the sententious *ars longa, vita brevis*—art is long, life is short, which may be described as one of the most influential opinions of all time, perhaps a proof in itself of its own validity.

In his *Advancement of Learning* (1605) Francis Bacon argues the benefits of disconnected sentences, or aphorisms, because he says this way of presenting knowledge stimulates further inquiry. Because an aphorism has to be compact and be without elaborate explanation or wearisome footnotes, only those who are what Bacon described as 'sound and grounded' are able to compose them.

As long as man has presented opinions in written form, aphorisms have been known: the books of Ecclesiasticus and the Proverbs of Solomon are just two Biblical sources of aphoristic knowledge. A great deal of modern opinion relies on the maxims and saws of the ancient Greeks, who may themselves have been influenced by hieroglyphic wisdom of the Egyptians. Latterly, of course, the French have brought the aphorism or the pensée to the prestige of an art form: the success of Pascal (*Pensées* 1660), La Rochefoucauld (*Maximes*, 1665), La Bruyère (*Caractères*, 1688), Vauvenargues (Introduction à la connaissance de l'esprit humain, 1746), Rivarol (1753-1801), Chamfort (1741-1794) and Joubert (1754-1824) may be judged by our familiarity with their opinions, centuries after they made them public. Cultivated in the salon of Madame de Sable or at the table of Chateaubriand, the aphorism evolved into the richest currency in the trade of thought.

Often, aphorists found value in detraction. It is too coarse to describe La Rochefoucauld as a cynic, although his great achievement was to illustrate so brightly the laughable hypocrisy and depressing small-mindedness of man. Pascal was not a simple misanthropist, even if his most famous *pensée* was that '*Tout le malheur des hommes vient d'une seule chose, qui est de ne savoir pas demeurer en repos, dans une chambre*—all human misery derives from man's inability to happily stay at home'. But he did memorialise the crassness and stupidity of his fellows.

Vauvenargues tried to be uplifting, but failed as a successful aphorist, even if today, after a lifetime of relative obscurity, the convention is to regard him as a major influence on Rousseau and the Encyclopaedists. A sardonic nature like La Rochefoucauld's is better suited to encapsulating the absurdity of man's ambitions. The wordliness of the French contributed greatly to their free play with wordiness and it is notable that England's great aphorist, Lord Chesterfield, a friend of Voltaire and Montesquieu, took his inspiration from abroad.

The modern opinion is a bastard form, part aphorism, part conviction, wholly personal, which has been greatly encouraged by an explosion of media. Ever since the rise of the interview as a staple of journalism, it has been increasingly necessary for those likely to be interviewed to have about them a useful set of opinions. Without opinions, personalities seem dull.

PERFUME

Perfume means simply 'from smoke' (Lat. *per fumum*), an etymology dependent on the first perfumes having been obtained by the combustion of aromatic woods and gums, once used to counteract the offensive odours of burning flesh in funerals and sacrifices. Now perfumes are more purely venereal. It is well known that odours are stimulants. Montaigne commented on it and so, more salaciously, did Robert Herrick in his poem 'On Julia's Sweat'. The smell of fenugreek is said, by experts, to resemble the smell of a woman's armpit, something which many men find powerfully erotic. Fascinatingly, the odoriferous agent in fenugreek is *cumarine* which also imparts the distinctive fragrance to new-mown hay. And here comes the fascinating bit: many women find the smell of new-mown hay reminiscent of semen.

Smell is a fugitive sense, but a very influential one. Artificial perfumes have the same sexual and aesthetic effects as natural odours. If you drew a map of the brain you would find that the olfactory bulb is in a suburb close to the temporal lobe, the place where we process time, the address of our memories. This propinquity explains the special power of smell to excite recollections of people and places when there is a cross-over in the senses. And of course this is the explanation of that mildly disturbing phenomenon, *déjà vu*. You have not necessarily been there before, but you can smell something which reminds you of someone or somewhere else. Sunshine and jasmine may recall Greece, the smell of chalk school. Maybe it was the smell of that madeleine that started off Proust. On a less lofty literary level, Richard Llewellyn, author of *How Green Was My Valley* (1939), claimed that he could smell hen's feathers every time he ate roast chicken.

But it is places rather than things which are most often recalled by smell. We lack a precise vocabulary to describe odour, having to take refuge in similes ('like strawberries or hay'), but its very elusiveness makes smell evocative. In *Small Talk* (1932), Harold Nicolson wrote unforgettable about the Edwardian weekend, using suggestions of smell, from the 'Hammam Bouquet of Mr Penthalicon' [sic] to the stuff that cleans around the bend, to create an historical atmosphere which is, at least, now fixed in my mind.

So powerful is the sense of smell that oenologists realise that the character of a wine is determined more by the nose than the tongue, and they are sometimes at odds with the biophysicists and gastronomes claiming precedence for one organ over the other in the empire of our senses. The complexity of the subject is suggested by flexibility of the vocabulary, few people making a precise distinction between smell, aroma, odour or perfume. (Apart from, famously, Nancy Mitford whose attack on the Frenchification of English for a while stigmatised 'perfume' and 'serviette'.)

Social confusion about what to call manufactured smell reveals an underlying technical imprecision in the subject. The fragrance industry depends on trying to put order on that mysterious and indefinable territory between subjective impressions and electrical activity in the neurones of the brain. While there are perfumiers, so evocatively described in Patrick Suskind's *Perfume* (1987), who can distinguish thousands of different odours, parosmia (an aberrant sense of smell) is not a rare disorder. Neurologists do not fully understand how the sense works, although it is known that molecules of odoriferous substances interact with certain cells in the olfactory bulb.

In his *Chimie du Gout et de l'odorat* (1755) Polycarpe Poncelet listed the seven tastes:

acide, doux, amer, piquant, fade, austere, aigre-doux

Currently, research into the mechanism of smell is attempting to isolate and identify the actual receptors, one theory being that—just as colour vision is mediated by red, green and blue—there are simply seven precisely definable chemicals which mediate the sense of smell.

It was in the 1860s that French parfumiers set about rationalising the industry, partly in response to the growth of the fashion business after Worth's creation of haute couture in 1858. In his book *Le Livre des parfums* (1870), Eugene Rimmel said there were six elementary odours: rose, jasmine, orange blossom, acacia, violet and tuberose. These refined floral odours were a fashionable reaction to heavier, animal scents such as musk, the rotted glandular secretions from *moschus moschiferus*, civet and ambergris, an intestinal calculus found in the rectum of the cachelot, whose crude erotic power the bourgeois found unsettling, while the libertine found attractive. The word musk comes from the Sanskrit term for testicles. Nowadays, six basic groups underpin male fragrances, each with its own characteristics. Viewed historically, it is clear that a taste for perfume fluctuates between floral and animal.

Huysmans' debauched hero, Des Esseintes, in *A Rebours* (1884), made the perfume-artist into a hero figure at exactly the same time that industrial production of soap and scent, and its distribution through the developing department stores, made perfume downwardly mobile. Thus it is extraordinary that the highest artistry in perfume was attained at exactly that moment when the mass-market was being realised. The unfinished story of perfume in the twentieth century is about the democratisation of luxury. Perfume does not mask stench, but suggests character. And packaging helps achieve this.

The history of the perfume industry is as much a history of packaging and design as it is of fashionable odour. Few products require the buttressing of packaging more than scent: by definition it is evanescent and it is therefore not surprising that the permanence of crystal—by René Lalique for Coty and Louis Sue for Lanvin—was early on required to lend solidity to the product. And the sharing of an image with that of a fashion designer, borrowing the style created by their particular kind of clothes, is an obvious way of reinforcing the character of a scent.

The history of civilisation could be written in terms of the sense of smell. Readers of Rabelais, Pepys or Defoe, know that one of the most striking impressions of cities in the past was the stink of the masses. In conditions of imperfect public health and hygiene, pre-industrial perfumiers were required to cover up human stench. (Although, according to the book of *Esther* in the Old Testament, members of the harem at Shushan had to be marinated in oil of myrrh for six months before being 'presented' to the king.) One gathers that this was for sexual rather than public hygiene reasons. Now the task is explicit statement, not disguise. Because the sense of smell is so little understood, it is the most exploited. Because it is so primitive, it is carnal. Lanvin once produced perfumes whose names with provocative subtlety placed them squarely in the sexual register: Scandale, Pretexte and Rumeur. Today, one of the most notable fragrances is called Obsession, again deliciously suggestive of sin. Now that the choice of any particular scent is a matter of free choice rather than hygienic necessity, this decadent preference is very revealing.

It is only a matter of time before manufacturers understand this more completely, providing ranges of fragrances to evoke not only sin, but places and people too. Coco Chanel said a woman should use perfume wherever she expects to be kissed, an echo perhaps of the Asian practice of perfuming the vulva, a practice favoured by the inhabitants of Sjeik Nefzaoui's harem.

*

PESSIMISTS

Are people who live with optimists.

PHALLIC SYMBOLISM

Aristophanes uses the following as metaphors of the penis: tip, eel, meat, muscle, dried fig, acorn, chickpea, pole, peg, ram, oar, beam, punt-pole, bolt, handle, sword, club, drill, sparrow, rope, lump, soup ladle (and, as a matter of interest, for the female: box, piggie, pomegranate, rose, garden, delphinium, meadow, thicket, grove, plain, celery, mint, fuzz, door, gate, circle, pit, gulf, vent-hole, sea urchin, conch, hearth, brazier, hot coals, boiled sausage, barleycake, pancake, nightingale, thrush, mousehole, bird's nest, swallow and gravy boat).

Contemporary French has the following affectionate terms: affaires personnelles, agace-cul, andouille à col roule, anguille, arbalête, arc, asperge, baguette, baigneur, balayette, bazar, bébête, bigoudi, bijou de famille, biniou, biroute, biscuit, bite, borgne, botte, bourre, bout, boute-joie, boutique, braque, braquemart, broquette, burette, calibistri, canari, canette, canne-à-papa, carabine, carotte, Charles le Chauve, cheville, chibre, chinois, chipolata, chopine, chopotte, cigare, clarinette, coco, coquette, coquin ravageur, cornemuse, créateur, dague, dard, dardillon, défonceuse, ecouvillon, epinette, fifre, flageolot, flêche, flûte, foutoir, frérot, fretillante, gaillarde, gaule, gland, goujon, goupillon, gourdon, guise, guiseau, histoire, lame, lavette, lezard, lime, macaron, manche, marsouin, moineau, Mont-Chauve, morceau, noeud, organe, os, os à moelle, outil, pain à lait, paf, panet, panoplie, paquet, petit-frère, petit jesus, petit oiseau, pine, pipe, pipi, piquet, pistolet, plantoir, pointe, poireau, poisson-rouge, polar, popol, précieuse, quequette, quille, rat-sans-pattes, ravissante, rossignol, saint-frusquin, saucisse, service-trois-pièces, tête chercheuse, thermomêtre-à-moustaches, -à-perruque, tige, tringle, trique, tromblon, trombone, trompe, trompette, truite, turlututu, vier, vit, zezette, zibar, ziogomar, ziozio, zizi, zob, zobi. And for testicles: accessoires, animelles, antilles, balles, balloches, ballottes, ballustrines, bandilles, basteaux, belaux, bijoux de famille, billes, binos, blatses, boulettes, bouteille a miel, brandilloires, breloques, bromborions, burettes, burnes, cliquailles, colei, compagnons, couilles, couillons, couple, cymbales, dandrilles, deux adjoints, deux bibelots, didymoi, genitoires, globes, gonades, gourdes, guenilles, guignes, histoires, instruments, joies de ce monde, joyeuses, jumelles, keilliou, landrilles, machines, maillaux, marjolles, marrons, noix, olives, olives de Poissy, paire, parties, pastrailles, patrimoine, pélotons, pendillantes, pendilloires, pendiloches, pendoires, pot-au-lait, pruneaux, prunes de Monsieur, reservoirs, ripons, rognons, roubignolles, rouleaux, roupettes, roustons, sac à avoine, sonnettes, tesniers pélus, testicules, trebillons, triqubilles, valseuses, vase spermatique, vessiés, virolets.

All organic forms, because of a short-circuit in the morphology-processing parts of the brain which connect the perception of curves to the idea of bodies, tend to evoke the phallus. Sexual symbolism dominates civilised life in all cultures. The phallus was central to Egyptian religion; the word itself comes from an ancient Semitic root *palash* which means 'to break through.' Quite so. The story of Jesus is a Judaeo-Christian gloss on older religions which practised phallic worship. The resurrection is just one version of ancient myths celebrating the sun just as Easter eggs are a survival of related pagan fertility cults. The Maypole is a phallic symbol. Should you get the chance to dance around one, you will not be taking part in a British Tourist Authority folkloric event, but participating in an ancient, savage rite which celebrates an aroused penis as a symbol of generation and continuity.

In architecture, sexual symbolism is so familiar that it is no longer tempting to make jokes about erections. Since Vitruvius the classical orders have been given a gender: slender Ionic columns were described as feminine, the more robust and simple Doric order was masculine. When in renaissance paintings of Mary Magdalene a cave appears in the background, it is a symbol of the womb. The elliptical halo—known as a *mandorla*—which often surrounds pictures of the Virgin and Child is a reference to the female genitals, whose external parts are 'the door of life'. In Dumblane Abbey there is a window, much admired by the innocent John Ruskin, whose symbolism is patently based on the *yoni*, that unforgettable shape which Mordecai Richler unromantically described as looking like a horse's collar. If you know what you are looking for, you can even see a clitoris; Ruskin (1819-1900), who famously became impotent on the shock discovery that women had pubic hair, remained oblivious.

Some authorities even claim that the familiar plan of the Christian church is based not on the architecture of Roman basilicas, but on the architecture of a woman's sex: you enter a church through double doors, a clear suggestion of the *labia maiora*; the porch is the *vestibula*; another pair of double doors are the *labia minora*; the nave is the *vagina* and the altar the womb. All of ancient myth and religion was based on anxiety about fertility which found expression in symbolic forms of the male and female sex organs. If we were going to start a new religion today it would be necessary to accommodate our anxieties not about fertility, but about *identity*. Again sex would play its part, but it is treacherous territory.

The 1958 Ford Edsel is famous as one of the greatest commercial disasters of all time. The manufacturer, mystified by the failure of a product that had been so meticulously developed, decided to do some after-market psycho-pathology in order to get to the bottom of the problem. The analytical techniques employed eventually revealed that, quite unconsciously, the vertical almond-shaped radiator grill of the doomed Edsel reminded a significant number of respondents of what, in more than four letters, might be described as a horse's collar. In private circumstances, a source of delight to most heterosexual men, God and Ford researchers alone know what depths of Jungian terror were plumbed by a thrusting V8 propelled chrome pussy leading two and a half tons of Detroit barge bowling down the turnpike.

Yet, to prove that both marketing *and* sexual symbolism are powerful, but imprecise instruments, just three years after the failure of the feminine Edsel, Jaguar's E-Type became an astonishing *succès d'estime* on account of a shape whose proportions—and even details—ape the penis. Renoir once advised young artists to 'paint with your dick!' The E-Type's designers simply allowed you to drive one.

There is a fascinating, but ill-researched, area of study relating the size of the nose to the size of the penis. The Romans believed in a strict relationship: Ovid observed '*noscitur a naso quanta sit hasta viro*', an observation courtesy of the Roman predilection for public bathing. This belief continued throughout the Middle Ages and in the Renaissance it developed into a more elaborate conviction that a law relating the size of the nose to the size and appetite of the sexual organs applied to women as well. In *The Emperor of the East* Philip Massinger writes:

> Her nose, which by its length assures me
> Of storms at midnight if I fail to pay her
> The tribute she expects.

PHILISTINES

The Philistines contested possesion of Palestine with the Israelites, hence a heathen foe. Thus: 'The Philistines be upon thee' (*Judges* xvi, 12). Its use to denote boorish, brutish manners was much popularised in England by Matthew Arnold's frequent employment of the term in his *Culture and Anarchy* (1869).

PICASSO

Picasso has always been a touchstone. In a brilliant essay in *Penguin New Writing* (1947), the sculptor Michael Ayrton said 'To write anything but praise, or to attempt anything but a favourable analysis of the present value and future significance of the art of Picasso, is to be attacked at once.'

Yet people do it. In a televised speech after the Royal Academy dinner in 1949 Sir Alfred Munnings said:

If I met Picasso in the street I would kick him in the pants.

Gertrude Stein's brother, Leo, said Picasso turned out 'Godalmighty rubbish'. When the Gestapo visited Stein's abandoned flat they found one of her Picassos and stuck a note on it saying 'Jewish trash, good for burning.' Norman Rockwell, the poet of suburbia, said his six-year-old granddaughter 'could do as well.'

Picasso can be magnificent and he can be trivial. In this sense he is a paradigm of Modern Art. Indeed, it was with his art that the crazy adventure of modernism began. All that is good and bad in twentieth-century painting is contained in Picasso's bravura declaration 'We didn't any longer want to fool the eye, we wanted to fool the mind.' While at once his art contains much for conservatives to mock (sculpture made of handlebars and cutlery), it also accommodates even more which commands respect: not least, restless invention, mischievous disrespect, and a continuous sense of wicked self-mockery. Were he not so sublimely talented and prolific, he might be a charlatan.

Certainly, there is an element of the mischievous god about him. One element of Picasso's super-abundant genius was his skill at phraseology. Often baffling, but nonetheless thought-provoking remarks such as: 'A picture is a sum of destructions' — something he told the art critic Christian Zervos in 1935.

Accordingly, Picasso has often been the target of fraudulent claims against his integrity, the most famous of which (purporting to be a confession of bad faith) was a fabrication by Giovanni Papini published (along with other fake interviews with Stendhal and Kafka) in *Il Libro Nero* in 1951. Although Picasso's distinguished biographer, Pierre Daix, exposed the fraud in *Les Lettres Françaises* in 1955, the careless and prejudiced have frequently repeated it. Still, Picasso himself believed that 'art and liberty, like the fire of Prometheus, are things one must steal.' His one-time collaborator, George Braque, who pursued a more consistent artistic direction, tired of the Picasso phenomenon and said 'Picasso used to be a great painter, but now he's a genius.'

Michael Ayrton explained: 'Picasso has required numerous art forms upon which to base his experiments. He is not concerned with ... a single tradition, and in this he differs from the artists of the past, as Woolworth's differs from the craftsman's shop.' It was a sort of artistic vampirism, marvellous, but false, a vast erection of bones in the graveyard of experience. 'Regarded without hysteria, it is surely plain enough that Picasso's constant, mercurial changes of style, which are today extolled as the fruits of a unique and all-embracing genius, are not a genuine development but superlative conjuring.' Picasso himself said 'I have a horror of repeating myself.' One man's repetition is another man's invention.

POLITICAL CORRECTNESS

While it may be true that opinions can only flourish in times when there is no dominant religious direction, it is perhaps also true that people with strong opinions may be seeking some sort of surrogate religious faith. This is surely the case with the alarming collective mania of political correctness. If an 'opinionated' person is an intransigent, dogmatic individual with scant regard for the nicer sensibilities of other folk, then political correctness may be seen to be the collective expression of an opinionated group. But the big flaw in political correctness is that, no matter how difficult or objectionable an opinionated individual may be, he is at least redeemed by being independent and singular in his cussedness. Political correctness hijacks brave opinions and turns them into an unthinking pallid orthodoxy.

The expression 'Political Correctness' was first used *ironically* by journalists to describe the reflex responses of fading left-liberal convention, mostly discredited, but still strong in certain areas of the media and on most campuses. PC is a gallimaufry of Summer of Love opinions, supported by a large body of decent liberal equivocation on any matter likely to cause offence to any recognisable group – other than wealthy WASPs or absolutely anybody with a conservative cast of mind, who are always fair game. Political correctness occupies the lower-middle ground of ideas, an uncontroversially packaged set of used opinions selected by their users to signal support for anything modish in modern life.

An intellectual is someone who enjoys the play and the misalliance of ideas. On the other hand, the politically correct point-of-view is naive and authoritative. Its intolerance and bigotry mocks rational ideas about genuine 'liberal' thought to which it is often mistakenly compared. The believer in political correctness cannot be an intellectual since he does not believe in the free play of ideas. He cannot even be a proper critic, since critics – whatever their politics – have to have intelligence *and* knowledge. The politically correct world is closed, it wants a fixed body of opinion, which is another way of saying that it is dead and irrelevant.

Language was the first victim of the PC adventure in mind control. First expressions of the politically correct mentality came a generation ago with the equal rights and feminist movements, although the vocabulary has been around a lot longer. Equal rights thinking required familiar expressions, most famously 'negro' to be replaced by 'black', held to be less demeaning (although, of course, semantically identical since 'negro' derives from the Latin root for the colour black). Negroes, especially hipster negroes, have subsequently shown their disdain for the fey PC intervention in manners by insisting on referring to themselves as niggers. Feminists used the same dungaree-clad, clod-hopping perversion of natural speech to create inelegant non-senses such as 'chairperson', 'chairman' being held to demean women. Soon, other sceptred minorities were given political correction so as to protect them from the assault of description or vilification by custom or convention. Thus homosexuals soon sought protection and queers became gays. The environment followed.

There is, of course, something queasily Stalinist about all this. All dictators, the Church included, detest experts since expertise suggests knowledge *and* opinion. While political correctness apes the conventions of liberal thought processes and pretends to the support of 'minority causes', it in fact represents a massive and complacent body of opinion. It:

Is against any independent or outspoken statement, even if supported by reasonable scientific data.

Is against any popular expression of an idea, except when that expression favours a group enjoying the support of the politically correct.

Is based on an orthodoxy of the same liberal opinion which has failed so catastrophically wherever it has been applied in economics and politics.

Is against individuals and prefers to support groups, from whom it demands uncritical devotion.

Is absolute and embittered. There are no shades or nuances of political correctness.

Does not exist to promote enlightened debate, but to impose

a stultifying and witless normalcy.

Is against humour and free expression.

Is for a glum and pallid consensus.

A small analysis of the term itself is interesting. PC is 'political' in that it aims to define a language (and, therefore, an approach) to social behaviour. In this respect it is authoritarian. It is 'correct' only in the most limited interpretation of that term.

So what defines political un-correctness? It is a willingness to form outspoken opinions on the basis of information and ideas offered without prejudice.

PORNOGRAPHY

Pornography is notoriously difficult to define, since to pursue it is to touch on assumptions about art, morals and much else besides. For instance, in his book *Early Erotic Photography* (1993) Serge Nazarieff convincingly demonstrated that the hugely respectable pioneers of French photography in the mid-nineteenth century ran lucrative undercover trades in pornographic images (as well as tasteful artistic nudes, registered at the Bibliothèque Nationale as study materials; those by the photographer Durieu had been used by Delacroix).

Auguste Belloc (d.1867), pioneer of the wet plate collodion process, author of scientific papers and a successful exhibitor at Crystal Palace in 1851, was a leading pornographer, as was Felix Moulin whose daguerrotypes of 'non-professional' teenage models cost him a month in prison and earned him the following commendation, circa 1850, from the Parisian police: 'so obscene that even to pronounce the titles … would be to commit an indecency.'

Behind the gently titillating scenes of soft-focus pubescent girls with vestigial breasts, half-clad as Bedouin maids, the same photographers practised a furtive trade in more explicit images with legs akimbo, gnarled dark bushes and unidealised pendulous, but impressive, breasts.

SAUCES

Ambrose Bierce was specially interested in sauces and in them he saw a measure of civilisation. A people with no sauces has one thousand vices, he said. A people who have, for instance, mayonnaise are left with only nine hundred and ninety-nine. The significance of sauce — whose source is the Latin word for 'salted' — is clear from the metaphorical frequency of the word and its various cognates. While a salty person is someone with a robust personality, a saucy person is altogether different. To serve the same sauce means to retaliate. 'Hunger' Shakespeare says 'is the best sauce.'

SALAD

The British, someone remarked, not being a spiritual nation, invented cricket to afford them some concept of eternity. This elegant conceit might be developed to read that the British, not being a nation of gastronomes, developed salads to enforce their conviction about the vileness of 'fresh' produce. British salad is a travesty of freshness, a misbegotten culinary salvage operation whose cumulative effect has undermined for generations the fragile appreciation of the relationship between raw food and healthfulness. In 1937 in Brooks', Geoffrey Madan heard someone say 'salad should be dry and tired: that's the great thing'.

The British believe that lettuce is insipid, savourless. The truth is more interesting. Medieval dieticians, who cultivated adversarial concepts of diet and its relation to personality, recognised that lettuce was cold and moist, the characteristics of the phlegmatic humour. So, in accordance with the theory, lettuce was not only recommended to cure temporary feverish conditions, but was also considered a suitable regulatory treatment for those with more permanent hot and dry choleric dispositions.

Far from being a boring, tasteless green leaf, lettuce is a

repository of powerful natural drugs: the medieval lettuce specially so. *Lactuca virosa* (wild lettuce) contains compounds such as lactuco-picrin, structurally similar to opium, with a genuinely narcotic quality. The herbalist, Thomas Culpeper, emphasised the soporific and anaphrodisiac qualities of lettuce, saying it 'abates bodily lust, represses venereous dreams.' In *Acetaria* (1699), his study of salads John Evelyn gives a vivid account of the power of lettuce: 'By reason of its soporific quality, lettuce ever was, and still continues the principal foundation of the universal tribe of sallets, which is to cool and refresh [and regulate] ... morall, temperance and chastity.' Sometimes known as opium lettuce, the effect of *Lactuca virosa* was familiar to Beatrix Potter's Peter Rabbit who says 'lettuces are very soporific', confirming a suspicion that the blameless creatures of Potter's tortured imagination were prey to unwholesome venerous dreams and articulate in coded language a colourful variety of suppressed opinions about sex and drugs.

Salads became debased as a consequence of industrialisation when processed food became available. The British were the first nation to be removed from the reality of the farmyard and field when peas and pork, for instance, began to appear in tins. The way industry urbanised the population and the way manufactured food distanced the suburban table from nature was as profound with plants-as-food (which is to say salads) as it was with meat. The classic salad – a robust forerunner of *salade niçoise* – was described by Alexandre Dumas in his posthumous *Le Grand Dictionnaire de Cuisine* (1873). To a manly collection of potherbs, including sorrel, lettuce, chard, orach, spinach and purslane, Dumas made a dressing with egg yolk and oil to which he added chervil, crushed tuna, macerated anchovies, Maille mustard, soya, chopped gherkins, egg whites and vinegar. The mixture was so dense that 'My servant tosses it', leaving Dumas only to cover the lot with a great deal of paprika and then eat it.

The British view is different, more delicate. According to Elizabeth David in *Summer Cooking* (1955): 'The grotesque prudishness and archness with which garlic is treated in this country has led to the superstition that rubbing the bowl with it before putting the salad in gives sufficient flavour. It rather depends whether you are going to eat the bowl or the salad.'

SIN

Elbert Hubbard, the twentieth-century Samuel Smiles, said 'We are punished by our sins, not for them,' *The Note Book* (1927).

There is no Biblical source for the notion of the Seven Deadly Sins. They became a Christian convention at about the time the Bible was being translated into European languages. Seven has always been a figure with special, mystical significance. For the Pythagoreans, the four and three which comprise it were lucky numbers. Creation took seven days, we have seven days of the week, seven ages of man and every seventh year is a sabbatical. There are seven candlesticks in the Apocalypse, and the seven churches of Asia (Rev. i, 11) are Ephesus, Smyrna, Pergamos, Thyatira, Sardis, Philadelphia and Laodicea.

The seven deadly sins are Christianity's reflection on man's weaknesses. With, perhaps, an eye to a significant mystery that goes back to the Babylonians, the same religious culture also gave us the Seven Stations of the Cross, the Seven Sorrows and Seven Joys of the Virgin and the Seven Works of Mercy. We owe it to Dante to have the seven deadly sins categorised. With poetical certainty, they were, our poet-guide tells us, arranged in the following order (the first being the most excusable, hence closest to Purgatory, or the Middle of the Road. The last was the most damning, therefore close to the pits of the Inferno, or eternity's very hard shoulder. Or maybe it should be in the other order):

Pride, Envy, Anger, Sloth, Avarice, Gluttony and Lust.

Of course, this is a culturally specific list. And, indeed, a somewhat dated one, as you would expect of someone whose courting began age eight and who was restricted to expressions of purity and tenderness—not progressing from hand-inside-the-blouse till seventeen. Or put it this way, from Dante's perspective, it was conventional to propose zeal as a counter-vailing virtue to sloth. Given the moral and practical damage generally wrought by the over-zealous, one thinks (although, in an erotic way, only for the briefest moment, of Donald Rumsfeld) most of us today would re-categorise sloth as the more virtuous characteristic.

But all the sins have their attractions: I am, for instance, extremely good at gluttony and pride. Even anger is wholesome. But lust is, of course, the most interesting. When he paraded personifications of the seven deadly sins before Faust in Marlowe's play, it was lust that Mephistopheles reckoned would turn the Doctor over. More recently, but over twenty years ago, Brigitte Bardot claimed to have had more than 5000 human sexual partners (this was before she became interested in animal 'rights' and wrongs). This, clearly, was prideful. And, compared to some people I know, at her age might even be evidence of an incipient inclination towards sloth.

As well as social, amatory and endocrinological, there are other psycho-medical explanations for lust, but they only go a part of the way as an explanation. It is true that damage to the amygdala, an almond-shaped part of the brain, can lead to an unquenchable desire for sex.

But, like seven itself, the whole thing is essentially a bit mysterious. Lust is clearly related to de Clerambault's Syndrome, sometimes known as erotomania. This is an obsessive-compulsive disorder where the sufferer has an intensely focussed sexual longing for another individual, one which is often not requited. It is related to nymphomania in

women and satyriasis in men. As a spoilsport, Freud explained
the latter (which takes the form of a permanent and unabatable
desire for sexual coupling) as a defensive reaction against
repressed homosexuality.

This sort of lustful libido is found not only in my own social
circle, especially so in married men of my age employed in the
arts and media, but also in severely regressed psychotics and
sufferers from temporal lobe epilepsy, where they are not the
same thing. The symptoms are familiar to many of us: a need to
masturbate excessively (however 'excess' may be defined —
Auden said the only reason we felt uncomfortable about
having a wank was that it can't be sentimentalised), to use
obscene gestures and to make gross and tasteless sexual
overtures at inappropriate moments. By that measure, almost
everybody I know has satyriasis. Nor are they seeking cures.

Lust is healthy. And universal (Baudelaire believed that
fucking was the lyricism of the unwashed). Take two
strikingly different examples, from a similar social milieu. The
very sporting Countess of Stafford, who died in 1932, felt she
was a little naive sexually so had the good sense to take
herself to a Parisian maison-de-passe for some instruction
before her marriage. On her wedding night her astonished
groom admonished her by saying 'Ladies don't move!' More
recently, Diana explained her Virginity by saying 'I knew I
had to keep myself tidy for what lay ahead.' There is
something utterly obscene and disgusting, sinful, in fact,
about that word 'tidy.' It would have been more wholesome if
the future Princess of Wales had admitted to a taste for same-
sex relations with cockatoos, possessing a world-class
collection of Murano glass dildoes, or declared a familiarity
with low bars in Toulon and maritime threesomes to follow,
or a liking for frottage in Camden Market with twelve-year-
old skateboarders and traffic wardens. That disgusting 'tidy'
is evidence of sinful pride.

SKIING

According to Harold Acton, communism de luxe.

STOCKMARKET

The economist Maynard Keynes said that when the capital development of a country becomes a by-product of the activities of a casino, the job is likely to be ill-done. And he added that the love of money as a possession — as distinguished from the love of money as a means to the enjoyments and realities of life — will be recognised for what it is, a somewhat disgusting morbidity, one of those semi-criminal, semi-pathological properties which one hands over with a shudder to the specialist in mental disease.

SUCCESS

Success is perhaps the single most despised achievement of an individual, what Ambrose Bierce called 'the one unpardonable sin against one's fellows.'

One modern definition of success is that when you get on an aeroplane, you should never turn right. Some American business theorists — inspired by work ethic rhetoric — believe that success is simply the result of (successfully) managing failure. They believe that 'failure contains tremendous growth energy.' Columbus discovered America by accident; Einstein discovered relativity when he (mistakenly) 'ignored an axiom'; Paul Gauguin was an unsuccessful stockbroker; Scrabble was invented after its creator, Alfred Butts, lost his job during the Depression. Quentin Crisp once remarked that if at first you don't succeed, failure may be your style. This idea is reflected in Tom Robbins' *Even Cowgirls Get the Blues* where he encourages us to 'Embrace Failure. Seek it out. Learn to love it. That may be the only way any of us will ever be free.' Robert Louis Stevenson believed 'Our business in this world is not to succeed, but to continue to fail, in good spirits.'

SURREALISM

From the Romantics through Freud to the Avant-Gardism of
the twentieth century, there has been a consistent tradition of
the artist as outsider, as the gifted seer and from that tradition
it is a small step to close the loop between art and madness.
Certainly, this was the case with surrealism, perhaps the most
popular of twentieth-century movements.

Surrealist artists and writers aimed, through a process
called automatism, to take a diversion around sanity and gain
a direct route to the sources of human desire and response. In
the case of Salvador Dali this was rather fraudulent as his
highly finished dreamscapes are, in fact, controlled by a
calculating and all too conscious ego: you have to be very
much awake to describe dreams in such fine detail. But in the
case of Antonin Artaud, the distance between artistic
expression and the ramblings and doodlings of crazed asylum
inmates is very small indeed. Artaud's last poem, written after
a busy session of electro-convulsive therapy, was called
Execration du père-mère and is, by most standards, absolutely
mad. To quote it in full makes the point well:

> o dedi
> o dada orzoura
> o dou zoura
> o dad skizi
> o kay a
> o kay a pontoura
> o pon oura
> a pena
> poni

Beauty, or, rather, 'convulsive beauty' was the key concept of
surrealism. Convulsive beauty was a term synonymous with
the 'marvellous', defined by Louis Aragon in *La Revolution
Surrealiste*, April, 1925 as 'la contradiction qui apparait dans le
réel.' Breton believed that the man who cannot imagine a

horse galloping on a tomato is an idiot.

In *L'Amour Fou* (1937) Andre Breton defines its three types: 1. mimicry. 2. the expiration of movement ('a photograph of a very handsome locomotive after it had been abandoned for many years to the delirium of a virgin forest.') and 3. the found object.

Surrealism questions the nature of reality. After Salvador Dali (whose name, Breton explained, was an anagram of 'Avida Dollars') Belgium's lugubrious René Magritte is the most popular Surrealist. His career began in advertising and shop display and his paintings depend as much on certain commercial techniques (the mise-en-page of isolated objects, the enlargement and exaggeration as in a sales catalogue) as they do on a subversive view of reality. There is something quintessentialy Belgian about Magritte (whose name is almost the same as Maigret's, Simenon's Belgian detective). Real subversives wear suits. Magritte's surrealism gives us a true vision of Belgium, a reminder that the real mysteries of the world are not the invisible ones, but the visible. Magritte tells us about the treachery of images … and so of course does advertising.

TASTE

The sensation in the mouth was perfectly described by Marcel Proust:

> But when from the ancient past nothing stands, after the death of beings, after the destruction of things, odour and taste alone survive, more fragile but more lively, more insubstantial, more persistent, more faithful: like spirits above the ruins of all the rest, they remain to recall, to await, to hope, and to bear unbendingly, in an almost inpalpable droplet, the immense edifice of recollection.

But it is metaphorical taste (that mixture of inherited

inclinations and acquired proclivities which find expression in social competition and cultural modelling) that is more interesting. There is a marvellous story that when asked what she thought about taste, Queen Elizabeth II replied 'I don't think it helps.' To Nietzsche 'all life is an argument about taste.' Nowhere is there more feeling and worse taste than a cemetery.

Taste is easier to detect than define, although it is certain that an awareness of the concept is a major element in the mechanisms of social distinction. When Dr Freud had middle-class Vienna supine on his couch circa 1900 he found that what troubled his patients most was sex. They wrung their hands about their relationships with their mothers, their fathers, their partners and their pets. From their agonies Freud concocted a fantastical and persuasive theory, inspired by classical mythology, which interpreted every human wish or act in sexual terms. The more you denied it, the more repressed Freud said you were.

Freud's theories may have been scientifically dubious, but they have won the century. So much so that all the inhibitions about sex which he so properly noted have now been released. Indeed, since Freud's liberation people are nowadays inclined to tell you perhaps rather more about their sexual experiences and preferences than you care to know.

A taboo is an unwritten law whose transgression brings shame. The modern taboo is taste. Taste is a merciless betrayer, occupying the dark side of the consumer's soul and constantly ready to make unsettling declarations about his education and his proclivities. The choices we make about the words we use, the gestures we employ, the environments we occupy, the clothes we wear and the things we buy articulate—often all too clearly—the source of our motivations.

The Romans had a concept of taste, but said there was no disputing about it: to any reasonable man, standards in art, manners, fashion and gastronomy were established by custom and it was simply a matter of training to understand them. This patrician attitude survived until the late eighteenth century (and remains the basis for all classical thought, whether expressed in architecture or any other medium), but the explosion in production and consumption which historians call the Industrial Revolution blew away the foundations of classicism. The question of taste arose when everybody became a consumer.

It's curious to remark that the idea of 'Good Taste' is itself vulgarly flawed because the self-conscious pursuit of gentility is, as it were, Bad Taste. Originally, 'Good Taste' found form in eighteenth-century French furniture, at least among people who hadn't been around the faubourgs of eighteenth-century France. Still in some quarters a sécretaire is the most reliable means of succinctly expressing a notion of artificial refinement: it is noteworthy that the first interior design fortune made in America was by the woman who introduced new American money to old French furniture.

UGLINESS

According to Serge Gainsbourg 'ugliness is superior to beauty because it lasts longer'. Ugly has a fascinating etymology, coming from the Old Norse *ugga*, to fear. This sense is preserved in the contemporary expression 'an ugly customer.'

Alas, the word ugsome, meaning revolting, is now obsolete. The Italian *'brutta figura'* does not even come close. In evident denial of a transcendent definition of 'beauty', the Poles believe there is no such thing as an ugly woman, only a lack of vodka.

VANITY

The most vain lines in all literature, or—at least—the most grandiose, belong to Sir Isaac Newton. The mathematician and astrologer responsible for what has been called the greatest generalisation of all time wrote at the beginning of his awesome *Principia Mathematica* (1687) 'Here I demonstrate the frame of the state of the Universe.' It might be conceded that one who made it his business to comprehend Universal mechanics might be allowed the odd, swaggering overstatement.

Smaller scale vanity is more commonplace. 'A continual feast of commendation is only to be attained by merit or wealth.' Dr Johnson and film-maker Marcel Pagnol knew that 'The most difficult secret for a man to keep is his own opinion of himself.' There are more aphorisms about vanity than any other human vice or virtue. Golda Meir is nicely heterodox: 'Don't be humble—you're not that great.' Equally, Oliver Wendell Holmes' remark makes double-bluffers insecure: 'Nothing is so commonplace as to wish to be remarkable.'

VENICE

Henry James said Venice was the easiest city in the world to visit without going there. However, 'When I went to Venice' Proust wrote 'my dream became my address.' Truman Capote said in 1961 that seeing Venice was like eating an entire box of liqueur chocolates in one go.

Venice was the first city to have street-lighting (in 1128 AD). It also gave us two distinctively refined contributions to contemporary culture: the ghetto as well as cutlery. There is a legend that it was the wife of an eleventh-century Doge who rejected the knife as a principal eating instrument in favour of an instrument with tines which we know as the fork.

The Venetian ghetto was founded on 10th April 1516 after Zacaria Dolfin, one of the Savi of the Collegio, had suggested that the Jews move into a separate area of the city and a part of the old northern parish of San Girolamo, famous as a cannon foundry, was recommended. Although the idea of separating Jews from Gentiles can be traced back to the Third Lateran Council of 1179, it was the ghetto of the sixteenth century which provided the world with a distinctive and notorious concept.

The etymology of the word itself is problematic. Some Jewish scholars say it derives from the Hebrew term for divorce papers, others from the Syriac word for community, or the Greek word for neighbourhood. 'Ghetto' is also temptingly near the Tuscan '*guitto*' and Modenese '*ghitto*' which both mean sordid, as well as to the German '*gehecktes Ort*', or hedged-in place, but it seems overwhelmingly likely that there is a specific Venetian origin. In the Venetian dialect, '*ghetto*' means foundry and as the Jews were required to settle in a parish where this trade was traditional, the inevitable association follows. Indeed, that the Jews moved into the '*ghetto nuovo*' rather than the established foundry area of the '*ghetto vecchio*', a Venetian rather than a Jewish origin is incontrovertible. Add to this that 'ghetto' also suggests a contraction of *borghetto*, Italian for 'little city' and the etymology of this most remarkable and sinister word seems secure.

Venice is stuck in reverse, the only city on earth going backwards. Clinging tenaciously to its past, contemporary Venice resists almost every intrusive threat of modernity — except, that is, tourism: the one that damages it the most. An English engineer called Nevile built a splendid iron bridge — modular components, very Prince Albert — at the Accademia in 1854. In a fit of wacky antiquarianism, it was replaced by a more 'appropriate' wooden bridge in 1932.

Venice is at once beautiful and sad, at the same time it is ancient, but sham. Venice to Edward Gibbon (1737-1794) was:

> Old and in general ill-built houses, ruined pictures, and stinking ditches, dignified in the pompous denomination of canals, a fine bridge spoilt by two rows of houses upon it, and a large square decorated with the worst architecture I ever saw.

Here Gibbon is echoing Dr Burnet in whose *Travels* (1687) we can read that there is 'nothing convenient' about the houses in

Venice and that the bread is 'extream Heavy ... the Crum is as Dough, when the Crust is as hard as a stone.' But Venice is now so fixed in the collective imagination that it is difficult to see it as it is, a magical city like the Arlequino character from the *Commedia dell'Arte* who looks happy and sad in turns. It is worth remembering that the fastidiously maintained decay is a lethal device of that Higher Tourism: Venice was a theme park before they invented the term. The streets may famously be full of water, but Ruskin's 'stainless waters proudly pure' now stink.

Just as Ruskin opposed the creation of the Buxton-to-Birmingham railway, he said between Windermere and Keswick a 'frenzy of avarice is ... blasting the cultivable surface of England into a treeless waste of ashes.' Applying this nihilistic and absurd rejection of wealth-producing, democratic travel to the Pearl of the Adriatic, Ruskin also fiercely opposed the creation of the vaporetto service to the Lido.

Henry James found the poverty useful for his art and conducive to his pleasure. In James we find the most eloquent expression of that retardataire snobbismo that has frozen Venice in the past. In 1872 he was complaining that the Lido was being 'improved' and the deserted beaches and dunes were turned into a mere 'site of delights' for visitors less worthy than The Master. These improvements, of course, comprised the Hotel Des Bains and the Hotel Excelsior we so admire today.

Privileged tourists like James wanted Venice kept in a state of picturesque poverty. He resented modern plumbing because this would deny him the sight of washerwomen struggling with huge ewers and pitchers. He resisted the industrialisation of glass making because it would reduce the number of bead-stringers whose back-breaking labour he enjoyed contemplating. While enjoying the luxury conveniences of The Danieli, James raged about the 'accursed whistling of the dirty steam engine of the omnibus to the Lido.' 'The misery of Venice' he said 'is part of the spectacle—a thoroughgoing devotee of local colour might ... say it was part of the pleasure.' To Henry James Venetian beggar girls looked at their very best when under-fed and wearing thin, exhausted, limp clothing; 'it would certainly make an immense difference if they were better fed.'

The fact that Venice is a fake was noted by the mad Futurist Marinetti who declared:

> We repudiate the Venice of the foreigners, market of antiquarian fakers magnet of universal snobbishness and stupidity ... We want to prepare the birth of an industrial and military Venice. Let us fill the stinking little canals with the rubble of the tottering, infected old palaces! Let us burn the gondolas, rocking chairs for idiots!

Marinetti was ignored. As a consequence Venice attracts 14m tourists a year, 10m of them day-trippers. The local population is perhaps 65,000. The four million who spend at least one night in Venice put enormous pressure on the remaining vernacular housing stock: there is a temptation that few have resisted to convert dwellings into small hotels and apartments for rent. In addition a third of Venetian dwellings are actually owned by foreigners and the natives are fleeing the place: they seek better amenities and, of course, the use of a car. Venice has only one supermarket.

WINE

Montaigne perhaps had the most *useful* attitude to wine. He said that if you base your pleasure on drinking good wine, you are bound to be disappointed by sometimes having to drink bad. 'To be a good drinker, you must not have too tender a palate.'

Despite attempts at obfuscation inspired by the trade, tasting wine is simple and all you have to do to acquire connoisseurship is to follow the technique taught by Victor Hazan. First hold the glass up to the light. Ask if it has brightness? Yes or no. What colour is it? Look at the meniscus. If there are signs of brownness it is old. Then sniff without agitating the liquid. What are the primary aromas? Then agitate the liquid. What are the secondary aromas? Drink a little. Is the taste long or short?

Tests like these inspire modern wine writers to acrobatic verbal pretension, especially as tastes are so notoriously difficult to describe. But few can improve on the following descriptions of white and red wine. The first from *The Green Man* (1969) by Kingsley Amis: 'a blend of cold chalk soup and alum cordial with an additive or two to bring it to the colour of children's pee' and the second by Robert Louis Stevenson 'as red as a November sunset and as odorous as a violet in April.' Wine writer Oz Clarke memorably described the taste of chenin blanc as being not unlike 'nuts and vomit'. Dylan Thomas said the wine distillate, grappa, 'tastes like an axe'. Here is a useful bluffer's guide:

Apple	Riesling
Apricot	Viognier (rare grape used in Condrieu, expensive white Rhône)
Asparagus	Sauvignon Blanc
Banana	Beaujolais
Biscuit	Champagne
Blackcurrant	Red Bordeaux (or any wine made predominantly from Cabernet Sauvignon)
Butter	Chardonnay
Cat's pee	Sauvignon Blanc
Cedar	Red Bordeaux
Cherry	Red Burgundy or Beaujolais; Italian reds
Chocolate	New world reds, the bigger Bordeaux and Burgundies

Farmyard	Red Burgundy
Game	Rhône
Gooseberry	Sauvignon Blanc
Grape	Muscat
Grass	Sauvignon Blanc
Honey	Chardonnay
Lemon	Any young white
Liquorice	Many reds
Lychees	Gewürztraminer
Mint	Cabernet Sauvignon
Nut	White Burgundy, Champagne
Oak	New World Chardonnays, Rioja
Peardrops	Young Italian whites
Pepper	Rhone
Petrol	Old Riesling
Plum	Any older reds
Raspberry	Beaujolais
Rose	Dry Muscat
Smoke	Pouilly Fumé, Pinot Grigio
Spice	Red Rhône and Alsatian whites
Strawberry	Beaujolais, red Burgundy, Rioja
Tar	Barolo
Tobacco	Red Bordeaux
Vanilla	Any wine aged in oak

OPINION-MAKERS

Flaubert had a list of opinion-makers—'Extraits d'auteurs
célèbres'. The best-known of these were Descartes, Condillac,
Chateaubriand, Dumas *fils*, the Goncourts and Lamartine, but
the list also included some rarities: Amedée Achard, Louis
Veuillot, Baume, Dupanloup, Mermillod and Claudia Bachi.

It is very easy to define an 'Opinion-maker'. They are the
writers whose opinions are better known than their books. They
tend to be quoted rather than read.

HAROLD ACTON 1904-1994

Harold Acton was the son of Arthur Mario Acton and of
Hortense Mitchell; he became a latterday Beckford or Walpole,
being both rich and talented enough to indulge his
dilettannteish interests without great embarrassment. His
American mother's fortune was used by his father to buy
property in Tuscany (notably the famous villa La Pietra),
although the family had long Italian connections: his
grandfather, Roger, left Naples for England. At Oxford he
announced his avant-garde credentials—to say nothing of his
stylised showmanship—by declaiming T.S. Eliot's *Wasteland*
through a megaphone. As one of the self-conscious Oxford

aesthetes of the twenties, Acton helped pioneer Oxford bags, a style of trouser whose indulgent cut was designed to distance its wearer from the sporting Hearties. Acton was immersed in Italy. His contemporary, Alan Pryce-Jones, said he was 'totally Mediterranean' and looked like a *condottiero* (although this exotic aspect may be attributable to a family story that Acton was an illegitimate descendant of the Rothschilds). His book, *The Last Medici*, was described by Pryce-Jones as 'an entertaining scrap of rococo history', although his *The Bourbons of Naples* was taken more seriously. His best book was his precocious autobiography, *Memoirs of an Aesthete*, although his enduring influence was as the doyen of a literary clique whose most famous figure was Evelyn Waugh. Acton—a bachelor— regularly received visitors, including the Prince of Wales, to La Pietra. Here he dispensed opinions about art and morals to the privileged. On Acton's death La Pietra was given to New York University. He is due to be exhumed shortly for DNA testing to settle the claim of his illegitimate half-sister for her 'legitimate portion' of the fortune.

WALTER BAGEHOT 1826-1877

Bagehot, through marriage to Elizabeth Wilson, daughter of the founder of *The Economist*, became the influential magazine's editor in 1860. The son of a banker, but trained as a mathematician, his 1867 book *The English Constitution* is one of the greatest of all political studies.

AMBROSE BIERCE 1842-1914?

Ambrose Bierce was the greatest—or, certainly, the most amusing—cynic of modern literature whose aphorisms have inspired a whole tradition in comic writing. He was born the youngest of nine children to a poor Ohio farmer and fought on the Union side in 1861. The Civil War was the laboratory where he developed his erudite cynicism. After the War as a journalist in San Francisco he wrote disturbing ghost stories *Can Such*

Things Be and *In the Midst of Life*, spent the years 1872 to 1876 in London and in Washington in 1900 wrote his masterpiece: *The Devil's Dictionary of Aphorisms*. In 1913 he went to Mexico to observe the rebellion and was never seen again.

CYRIL CONNOLLY 1903-1974

Cyril Connolly is famous for having been able to cry tears of boredom *at will*. His literature looks insignificant, but his influence was considerable. Born in Coventry, the child of a soldier and an Irish cowman, he was a contemporary of George Orwell's at prep school. He went to Eton and Balliol on scholarships. His novel, *The Rock Pool*, was published in 1936, a mannered study of the artsy decadence of the Cote d'Azur. A committed modernist, despite his thoroughly conservative demeanour, Connolly founded the influential *Horizon* in 1939 and became its editor in 1950. He was a well-used literary critic in the quality papers of his day, especially *The Sunday Times*, *The Observer* and *The New Statesman*. Connolly's other books include *Enemies of Promise* and *The Unquiet Grave*, but his great influence as an opinion-maker was, throughout the fifties and sixties, the voice of modern authority on literary matters in the better Sunday papers.

R.W. EMERSON 1803-1897

Emerson is never, ever, read, but references to and quotes from him still fill dictionaries of quotations and anthologies of aphorisms perhaps because his pan-Atlantic career made him suitable plundering ground for anthologists in both Britain and America. After Harvard he was briefly a pastor in Boston before sailing to Europe in 1832. His books include *Nature* (1836), *Essays* (1841), *Poems* (1846) and *English Traits* (1856).

BALTASAR GRACIAN Y MORALES 1601-1658

Gracian was the author of many apothegmatic works and creator of ambitious literary theories. His *Oraculo Manual* was a favourite of Schopenhauer. In this guide to life and manners, which has been described as a work of systematic misanthropy, he articulates his belief in the benefits of '*disengano*' or disengagement from the world.

CLEMENT GREENBERG 1909-1994

Greenberg, born in the Bronx, was the American art critic who helped to bring credibility to Jackson Pollock and the whole school of Abstract Expressionism as an artistic movement. This was perhaps a consequence of his particular psycho-social circumstances. Greenberg's parents rejected his artistic efforts as a child, destroying his drawings. He later described them as 'barbarians'. Hunger being the best sauce, this gave him an avid taste for pictures and was perhaps a source influential theories on the mutual antagonism between artists and the average person. Greenberg began writing for *The Partisan Review* while employed as a federal Government customs clerk. This gave him entry to the self-conscious world of the New York intelligentsia who, during the fifties of the last century, saw the promotion of abstract painting as part of their programme. His breakthrough essay was 'Avant-garde and Kitsch' which appeared in 1939. He has been described as the most influential art critic ever. Always willing to offer an opinion — Michelangelo was 'damned good, but was too arty' — Greenberg became as famous as the artists he championed. He was also the butt of hostile criticism, known as 'Clembashing'.

SAMUEL JOHNSON 1709-1784

After Shakespeare, Johnson is probably the most quoted individual in English literature. His thought is based on majestic scholarship, huge appetites, a beautiful literary style, a pervasive melancholy and a trenchant sense of irony. His writing began with the *Voyage to Abyssinia* of 1735, a narrative fantasy now reminiscent of Rousseau or Voltaire, but his masterpiece was the compilation the *Dictionary of the English*

Language (1755), a Faustian task which has become a standard of world literature. Johnson was a complex individual, given to bouts of lethargy and industry. His journal, *The Idler* (1761), captured that mood.

CARL GUSTAV JUNG 1871-1961

Jung is a paradigm of the author more quoted than read. His theories of collective unconscious, inspired by close study of myth, religion and folklore, are now seen as a persuasive alternative to Freud's more internalised sexual theories of human motivation (although they were once considered cranky). Jung's books include *The Theory of Psychanalysis*, *Psychology and Religion* and *Man and his Symbols*.

H.L. MENCKEN 1880-1956

American philologist, editor and satirist, born at Baltimore, became a journalist and literary critic. Satirical, individual and iconoclastic, he greatly influenced the American literary scene in the twenties. In 1924 he founded the *American Mercury*, and his great work, *The American Language*, was first published in 1918.

WILLIAM MORRIS 1834-1896

William Morris, son of a rich city sharedealer who made his fortune from the mindless toil and drudgery of a Devon copper mine, was the spirit of the Arts and Crafts Movement. As a designer of wallpaper and a prosperous, bearded, philandering, pamphleteering, proselytizing socialist, Morris was a fine prototype of the chattering classes. Morris repudiated the industrial achievements of the nineteenth century — contemptuously ignoring the fact that they had allowed him to inherit his wealth — and imagined a fanciful dreamworld of puerile medievalism. He was a designer of flat patterns (wallpaper and fabrics) of real skill and a furniture designer of great synthetic charm. His poetry was, however, despicably bad. A sojourn in Iceland in 1871 made it worse. He translated sagas. In 1877 Morris founded the Society for the Protection of Ancient Buildings, the scriptural beginnings of the conservation movement which then retarded British culture.

BLAISE PASCAL 1623-1662

Pascal was a mathematician of genius—publishing a theory of conic sections at sixteen and developing his own computer three years later. In 1654—rather like Isaac Newton—he had a religious revelation perhaps brought on by his failing scientific inspiration. He dallied with the Jesuits. His *Lettres provinçiales* were published in 1656 and two years later followed his celebrated and beautiful *Pensées*.

GAIUS PLINIUS SECUNDUS c. A.D. 23-79

Pliny was the author of *Naturalis Historia*, an encyclopaedia. This work originally consisted of thirty-seven volumes in which he claims to have stated 20,000 facts, gathered from some 2000 books and from 100 select authors.

FRANÇOIS DE LA ROCHEFOUCAULD 1613-1680

La Rochefoucauld's *Réflexions, ou sentences et maximes morales,* appeared in 1665 after a life of fighting and intriguing. Like a great wine, they have structure, great character and a certain asperity. They also have great wit and an aimiable patrician cynicism. The follies of self-love were one of La Rochefoucauld's preoccupations : 'vanity' he observed 'is a worse slanderer than malice'.

JOHN RUSKIN 1819-1900

Ruskin was the last Hebrew prophet. The library edition of his complete works has more than three thousand index references to the Scriptures. Ruskin was the magnificently paradoxical moralist of Victorian art and letters. The privileged—and somewhat overwrought—son of a wealthy wine merchant, Ruskin suffered a childhood whose strict religous discipline (paintings were turned to face the walls on Sundays) enhanced his appetite for art. A complex figure – the champion of Turner, the antagonist of James McNeill Whistler – the orotund Biblical cadences of his prose style are one of the great monuments of nineteenth-century English prose. Certainly, they were ideally suited for Ruskin's purpose of restoring moral integrity to art. Equally, his opinions were so forcefully held and persuasively expressed they brooked little opposition. When he described the Duomo at Siena as 'over-cut, over-striped, over-crocketed, over-gabled, a piece of costly confectionary and faithless vanity' few were prepared to disagree. Ruskin's great books were *Modern Painters* (1843), *The Seven Lamps of Architecture* (1848), *The Stones of Venice* (1851) and *Praterita* (1885-1889).

Art was not sufficiently large a subject to contain all of Ruskin's moralising and reforming energy. His opinion that art has a moral character was inevitably to lead to his interest in political economy. His tenure as Slade Professor of the Fine Arts at Oxford gave him many opportunities to develop his taste for righteous work: he once made a group of undergraduates go road-mending. It is thought that Ruskin became impotent when he discovered, through the good offices of his wife, Euphemia Chalmers Gray (who subsequently married the Impressionist painter John Everett Millais), that women had pubic hair. An indefatigable supporter of Gothic architecture (which in his opinion was good) and a tireless opponent of the classical (which was bad), Ruskin was a conservative whose thought helped lay the basis for modern architecture. He went mad.

GEORGE SANTAYANA 1863-1952

The Spanish born American philosopher, poet, novelist and international boulevardier became professor at Harvard in 1907. His writing career began as a poet with *Sonnets and Other Verses* (1894). A man of some style – described as 'suave, meticulous and seldom excited' — it was said that even in country lanes he wore patent-leather button boots. A few days before the city's capture seemed imminent Santayana told Bertrand Russell: 'I think I must go to Paris, because my winter underclothes are there, and I should not like the Germans to get them.' Although first published as a poet, he became known as a populariser of philosophy; Russell said he could never take him seriously. Santayana is never, ever, read — at least, not nowadays — but often quoted. You cannot turn up a volume by Logan Pearsall Smith and not find references to this Spanish sage. Not quite a twentieth-century Gracian, Santayana — from the lounges of the leading hotels of the world — presented the great moral and aesthetic debates of the modern world in a style which intellectual snobs could accept and which common people could still understand. 'Culture' he believed 'is on the horns of dilemma : if profound and noble it must remain rare, if common it must become mean.'

GERTRUDE STEIN 1874-1946

Gertrude Stein published the first recipe for hash cookies. She studied philosophy and psychology at Radcliffe under William James, Henry's brother and author of the influential *Varieties of Religous Experience*. She lived largely in Europe, published *Tender Buttons: Objects, Food and Rooms* in 1914 and *Wars I Have Seen* in 1945. Committed at once to Europe, modernism and lesbianism, Gertrude Stein was a fixture on the American arts circuit in Paris, dispensing criticism, advice and opinions from her rue de Fleurus (and later rue Christine) apartment to, among others, a young Ernest Hemingway (who humbly acknowledges her influence in *A Moveable Feast*). Her companion was Alice B. Toklas.

MARQUIS DE VAUVENARGUES 1715-1747

Luc de Clapiers, the second Marquis de Vauvenargues, was

born at Aix-en-Provence. Poor-health made him. He began to record his reflections on life and in 1746 his *Introduction à la connaissance de l'esprit humain, suivie de réflexions et maximes* was quietly published in Paris. To achieve great things it is necessary to believe you are going to live forever was his most popular opinion — though he died at thirty two, not knowing anything of his literary celebrity. After the 1857 edition of his *Introduction à la connaissance*, Vauvenargues in fact became immortal (although no one ever painted his portrait).

GORE VIDAL 1925

Elegant, patrician, but increasingly cranky, Vidal has outlived all but his most tenacious rivals for the title Grand Old Man of American literature. Vidal has used his connections — a Kennedy here, a senator there — tirelessly. He wrote the script for Ben Hur and his black comedy *Myra Breckinridge* was a pioneer study in trans-gender subject-matter. Subsequent novels have been less noteworthy, although his stature as a witty opinion-maker is peerless : 'I suspect one of the reasons we create fiction is to make sex exciting'.

EVELYN WAUGH 1903-1966

Evelyn Waugh, born above a Hampstead dairy, but forever aspiring to more lofty positions, was the greatest English comic novelist of the twentieth century. But while *Decline and Fall* (1928) and *Brideshead Revisted* (1945) are unforgettable masterpieces, Waugh exerted an influence beyond his considerable literary achievements. A Catholic convert from 1930, his waspish humour and famously acerbic manner — his first remark to a terrified young interviewer was 'I want a crème de menthe' — defined an ambitious and romantic spirit of reaction. Waugh enjoyed stylizing his adroit buffoonery, in whose bitterness and calculated wickedness there is the source of opinions which may prove to be even more lasting and relevant than his novels.

OSCAR WILDE 1854-1900

Wilde, the son of a fashionable Dublin dentist, is one of the greatest wits in English and, after Shakespeare and Johnson, the most quoted author in English. A keen transatlantic traveller, he found the Atlantic 'disappointing'. *The Importance of Being Earnest* appeared in the same year he was sentenced to two years in Reading Gaol for his 'illegal' relationship with Lord Alfred Douglas. He went to live in Paris and converted to Catholicism. He died in Paris, at what is now L'Hôtel where he said 'either this wallpaper has to go or I'.

EDITH WHARTON 1862-1937

A patrician New Yorker, brought up in France. She published *Fast and Loose,* a novel, at fourteen; *Verses* when sixteen. In 1885, she married Edward Wharton and divorced him six years after having moved to Paris in 1907. *Ethan Frome* (1911), *Custom of the Country* (1913), *The Age of Innocence* (1920) followed. But perhaps more influential than her novels was the 1897 *Decoration of Houses.*

TOM WOLFE 1931

Tom Wolfe, with Gay Talese and Hunter S. Thompson, the vanguard of the 'New Journalism', was, unlike his colleagues, neither a slick metropolitan nor a desperado drug-addict. Instead, he was a southern gent whose interest in popular culture came as much from an anthropologist's fascination as from a very particular desire to be or be seen to be hip. Wolfe made street life a respectable subject for articulate journalism and invented a language appropriate to it. His favoured leader dots '...' said by him to be born of frustration at not finding the right word, were also used by Nathalie Sarraute who called them *'points de suspension'.*

Wolfe, however, has been more influential. He is fascinated by heroes and, in a satiric style influenced by Thackeray, enjoys mocking the foibles and pretensions of the rich and powerful. After two decades of writing some of the most influential non-fiction of the sixties and seventies, including hilarious conservative attacks on modern art and architecture, Wolfe has made a persuasive case for the realistic novel. His *Bonfire of the Vanities* was published in 1988 and, using many of the techniques of New Journalism (close observation, fantastical exaggeration, sardonic humour and impressionism), may yet be considered what his critics always deny him: the Great American Novel. Wolfe's earlier books include: *The Kandy-Kolored Tangerine-Flake Streamline Baby* (1965), *The Electric Kool Aid Acid Test* (1965), *Radical Chic* (1970), *The Painted Word* (1975), *The Right Stuff* (1979) and *From Bauhaus to Our House* (1981).

ELSIE de WOLFE 1865-1950

Elsie de Wolfe was an unsuccessful showgirl (her first job was with Charles Frohman's Theatre Company in New York and she learnt to speak French on the Paris stage) who virtually invented the interior design profession. In 1903 she bought the Villa Trianon at Versailles, just before she gave up acting for decoration. Her book, *The House in Good Taste*, was published in 1913, establishing the term in English. Her first major commission was the interior design of New York's Colony Club: here white trellis became a trademark. Later, she designed an apartment for Condé Nast's daughter, Natica, making the link between fashion magazines and interior design which lasts today. Not only did she have a stirring personal aesthetic — 'plenty of optimism and white paint!' was one of her mottoes — which gave direction and credibility to her business, but she also defined many of its foibles. One, she became a cheerful homosexual. Two, she established an extreme solipsism ('Ah! It's beige. *My* colour' she said on seeing the Parthenon). Three, she had lofty social aspirations, becoming Lady Mendl in 1926 when she married Sir Charles, an amiable minor English diplomat well-known on the Côte d'Azur.

Dictionnaire des IDEES REÇUES

by

Gustave Flaubert

THUNDER AGAINST!

BY STEPHEN BAYLEY

'Thunder against' was Gustave Flaubert's ironic advice to anyone in search of a conformist response to the taxing issues of the day. The nineteenth-century consumer demanded manufactured opinions as much as he demanded mass-produced gas mantles. A stultifying corruption of free-thinking was the result of the former as surely as vulgarity in design was a result of the latter. Flaubert loathed the lazy complacency of middle-class opinions and taste and made it the subject of his last novel. The very odd *Dictionnaire des idées reçues*, a list of topics with opinionated definitions, was a supplement to the posthumous novel *Bouvard et Pécuchet*. Each is a ruthless satire on middle-class opinion. Flaubert attached a high significance to *Bouvard et Pécuchet*, thinking it perhaps his greatest work, but few critics have agreed with his own estimate of its worth.

While Flaubert wanted to ridicule the lazy clichés of nineteenth-century thought, he is not innocent of fault himself. Much of *Bouvard et Pécuchet* and the *Dictionnaire* is boring repetition of Flaubert's own tastes and prejudices, thus — consciously or not — he demonstrates the folly he intends to ridicule. And in the *Dictionnaire* itself, it is far from clear exactly what status Flaubert accords the various entries. Are they mockery or are some sly and knowing? At what level are we to understand its bluff certainties? To demonise an idea is, at the same time, to legitimise it. Is the *Dictionnaire* addressed to the reader from the author? Or is it an imaginative supplement provided by our two clerks, compiling their garbage mountain of useless knowledge?

A weasely Sartre called *Bouvard et Pécuchet* 'colossal and grotesque … vast and monotonous.' The *Dictionnaire* is none of those things, but it is unforgettable. Like *Bouvard et Pécuchet*, it is incomplete and hopelessly flawed. And like *Bouvard et Pécuchet* it is fascinating. The Francophile critic Cyril Connolly, a more sympathetic reader than the St Germain Existentialist, described *Bouvard et Pécuchet* as a 'post-symbolist Bible whose music still haunts us like a baying hound'. That's much more like it. The haunting quality of the *Dictionnaire* is unmistakable. Indeed, once you have read the *Dictionnaire*, a pattern of thought is set in your mind forever:

DICTIONNAIRE: a prop for the incuriously inquisitive,

a pretentious volume.

You get into the mood and mind of Flaubert, doing as he did, cataloguing opinions and then offering an opinion on these opinions. Even as he compiled it, Flaubert must have been uncomfortably aware of all the levels of ambiguity and futility in such a task. His precise relationship to his material remains unclear. If your subjects are human ignorance and vanity, you immediately enter a double bind in describing or cataloguing them. Equally, the subject is endless and indefinable.

The bibliographic history of the *Dictionnaire* is muddled although it is clear that it was always intended to be an addendum to *Bouvard et Pécuchet*. The novel describes two clerks, one fat, the other thin, who tire of the routine copying required of their calling and decide, instead, to acquire all the world's knowledge and publish it as an encyclopaedia of human ignorance. At one stage they become interested in faience soupières, at others in pregnancy, constipation and life expectancy. *Bouvard* and *Pécuchet* are the very prototypes of Sartre's own ludicrous autodidact, models for ambitious twenty-first-century man.

Bouvard et Pécuchet has been described as a prosecutor's address, designed to offend Flaubert's despised bourgeoisie. The anthology of encyclopaedic fact and stupidly conformist opinions the diligent clerks are assembling was described by A.J. Krailsheimer in his 1976 translation of *Bouvard et Pécuchet* as 'ritual word-play ... clichés, social noises'. This a perfect definition of the *Dictionnaire* itself. It was meant, in Flaubert's acid description, to be '*tout ce qu'il faut dire en societé pour être un homme convenable et aimable*'. Or, in other words, exactly what Flaubert detested. Yet he was obsessively dedicated to it himself. He read more than one thousand five hundred books to prepare for *Bouvard et Pécuchet*, an effort which accelerated his own demise in 1880. But just as the clerks failed to find the certainties they wanted and had, instead, to settle for idiocies, so Flaubert agonisingly said of his own satirical efforts to acquire all knowledge that in the end the result was: '*Je doute de tout, et même de mon doute*'.

Thus there is a deep and confusing ambivalence about the material. While the *Dictionnaire* was conceived in the late 1840s (it is first mentioned in a letter of 1850), from boyhood Flaubert had enjoyed collecting opinions, often recorded from his parents' visitors' mutterings; the more foolish the better.

There is an old French intellectual tradition of this: a 'sottisier' is a catalogue of stupidities. 'Bêtise' is an untranslatable word for silliness. Each term is still current in France. Flaubert was not alone in feeding popular taste for opinions. In 1879, for instance, *Le Parfait Causeur* offered its readers an easy introduction to the world of elegant ideas and in the same year Eugene Vivier published *Très peu de le qu'on entend tous les jours*. The gastronome Curnonsky's *La Musée des erreurs* is another example of the genre. There was a subsidiary purpose for Flaubert in compiling his own sottisier: many of the entries eventually published in the *Dictionnaire* were originally sources for details in his great novels. The entry on 'Actrices', for instance, finds its way into *Madame Bovary*.

Bouvard et Pécuchet was published incomplete in 1881 with a preface by Guy de Maupassant. The manuscript of the *Dictionnaire*, a mere forty folios, was only discovered in 1910 by E.L. Ferrere, while researching Flaubert's aesthetics, the year Louis Conard published *Bouvard et Pécuchet* in the *Oeuvres complètes de Gustave Flaubert*. The *Dictionnaire* first appeared as a separate volume in 1913. It fascinated Ezra Pound who wrote on 'James Joyce et Pécuchet' in the *Mercure de France* in 1922. Joyce's *Ulysses*, of course, has its own chapter of clichés. In 1946 the French writer Raymond Queneau provided a new ending for the incomplete *Bouvard et Pécuchet*. A private press produced a translation of the *Dictionnaire* in London in 1954, the same year Jacques Barzun published his translation; *Bouvard et Pécuchet* (the novel) became a Penguin Classic in 1976 and in 1994 a miniature edition of the *Dictionnaire* was published in Paris by Mille et Une Nuits.

Flaubert's *Dictionnaire* is an account, necessarily incomplete, of the ritual responses of the unreflecting Second Empire bore. Inevitably, little of it makes sense to us today. Too many of the references are inaccessible and many of the jokes were weak even in their own day. But as an idea, as 'the great monument of Flaubert's scorn', in Philip Toynbee's words, the idea keeps on resonating. At the end of the sketchy *Dictionnaire* there is an even more flimsy 'Catalogue des idées chics' supported by 'Extraits d'auteurs célèbres'. One of these 'celebrated' authors was La Harpe whose opinion on Shakespeare Flaubert takes to be notably idiotic: '*Shakespeare lui-meme, tout grossier qu'il etait, n'etait pas sans lecture et sans connaissance*—Shakespeare, who was quite coarse, nonetheless did not entirely lack education and learning.'

It is easy to imagine similar opinions passed with deadly solemnity around the dinner tables of Flaubert's provincial Rouen. In a letter to George Sand of 1871 Flaubert said that 'all our trouble comes from our gigantic ignorance'. And as he worked on acquiring remedial knowledge, it became increasingly clear that vast accumulations of vital knowledge were as futile and worthless as vast deposits of torpid ignorance. The compilation of the *Dictionnaire* was a giant leg-pull, but its effect was probably unclear to Flaubert himself. As a castigation of cliché, it is only a partial success. A 'cliché' is, actually, a set of words so familiarly used together that printers did not break up the composition of type. But even in the *Dictionnaire* Flaubert has clichés of his own. The expression '*Tonner contre*', his facetious advice to 'thunder against it', appears repeatedly, as does '*On ne sait pas ce qu'est* — whatever it is'. You can sense, in the latter, his own mounting despair with his task.

Bouvard et Pécuchet and the *Dictionnaire* are not merely satires of the bourgeois and his lust for conformist opinion, they are also allegories of the entire nineteenth century. The intellectual 'cliché' which is Flaubert's subject is a symbol of the new industrial systems and communications technologies which turned images, ideas and information into mass-produced commodities. The more there were, the less they were worth. This is a tragic critique of the modern world. Cyril Connolly's description of *Bouvard et Pécuchet*, which he included in his *One Hundred Key Books of the Modern Movement*, (1965), works perfectly for the *Dictionnaire* itself: 'Polymath pessimism ... irradiated by gleams of poetry: slapstick fused with the sadness of things'. Knowledge and ignorance baffled even Flaubert. '*Et la fin du jour se passa dans les incertitudes, les regrets ...*' The only thing to do is to thunder against.

A

ABELARD: Not necessary to have the slightest understanding of his philosophy or even knowing the title of his works. Make a discreet allusion to the injury inflicted upon him by Fulbert. [Heloïse's uncle who had him castrated] The tomb of Heloïse and Abelard: if someone proves to you that it is a sham, cry out: 'You are robbing me of my phantasies!'

ABRICOTS—Apricots: We won't be having any more of them this year.

ABSALON—Absalom: If he had worn a wig, Job wouldn't have been able to kill him. A facetious name to give to a bald friend. [The third son of David was killed while hiding in a tree]

ABSINTHE: Very violent poison: one glass and you're dead. Journalists drink it while writing their articles. Has killed more soldiers than the Bedouins.

ACADEMIE FRANCAISE—French Academy: Run it down but try to become part of it if you can.

ACCIDENT: Always deplorable or tiresome, as if one could ever consider a misfortune to be a cause for rejoicing.

ACCOUCHEMENT—Pregnancy: A word to avoid; replace by event. 'When is the [happy] event expected?'

ACHILLE—Achilles: Add 'fleet of foot': this gives the impression that you have read Homer.

ACTRICES—Actresses: The ruin of sons of [good] family. They are terrifyingly lecherous, indulge in orgies, consume millions, end up in hospital. I beg your pardon! Some of them are good mothers of [good] family.

ADIEUX—Farewells: Speak of the farewell at Fontainebleau with a catch in your voice. [Where Napoleon departed for Elba]

ADOLESCENT: Never start a prize-giving speech other than by saying 'Young adolescents' (which is a pleonasm).

AFFAIRES (LES) — Business matters/love affairs: Come before all else. A woman must avoid talking about hers. The most important thing in life. Affect everything.

AGRICULTURE: One of the breasts of the state (the state is of masculine gender but never mind). Should be encouraged. Short of workers. [The 'breast' image comes from Sully, Henri IV's minister]

AIL — Garlic: Kills intestinal worms and puts one in the mood for amorous conquest. Was rubbed on the lips of Henri IV at the moment when he was born.

AIR: Be careful of draughts. Without exception, currents of air run opposite to the temperature: if it is hot, they are cold, and vice versa.

AIRAIN — Brass: Metal of Antiquity. [Flaubert is dissing the ignorant who were confused by ancient bronze and more *arriviste* brass]

ALBATRE — Alabaster: Used to describe the most beautiful parts of a woman's body.

ALBION — England: Always preceded by white, perfidious, positive. Napoleon all but conquered it. Elegise it: free England. [The expression 'Perfidious Albion' was coined by Napoleon in 1803]

ALCIBIADE — Alcibiades: Famous for his dog's tail. Debauched type. Went round with Aspasia. [Nephew of Pericles, apple of Socrates' eye, had his dog's tail cut off to enrage Athenians and distract attention from his philandering]

ALCOOLISME — Alcoholism: Cause of all modern illnesses (see Absinthe and Tobacco).

ALLEMAGNE — Germany: Always preceded by blond, dreamy. But what military organisation!

ALLEMANDS — Germans: A nation of dreamers (*old-fashioned*). It's not surprising that they beat us, we weren't ready!

AMBITIEUX — Ambitious: In the country, any man who gets himself talked about. 'I'm not ambitious!' means selfish or incompetent.

AMBITION: Always preceded by blind unless it is noble.

AMERIQUE—America: A good example of injustice: it was Columbus who discovered her, but she takes her name from Americ Vespuccio. Without the discovery of America we wouldn't have syphilis or phylloxera. Praise her all the same, especially if you've never been there. Rant about 'self-government'.

AMIRAL—Admiral: Always brave. Only swears on a thousand scuttles.

ANDROCLES: Mention Androcles' lion in reference to lion tamers. [Runaway slave befriended by a lion after pulling a thorn from its paw]

ANGE—Angel: Does well in love and literature.

ANGLAIS—Englishmen: All rich.

ANGLAISES—English women: Be amazed by what pretty children they have.

ANTECHRIST—Antichrist: Voltaire, Renan… [Virulent anti-clerics]

ANTIQUITE—Antiquity, and everything connected to it: Clichéd, annoying.

ANTIQUITES (LES)—Antiques: Always of modern fabrication.

APLOMB: Always preceded by devilish or brazen.

APPARTEMENT DE GARCON—Young man's digs: Always in a mess, with ladies' bits and pieces here and there. Smells of cigarettes. You will find extraordinary things there.

ARBALETE—Crossbow: Good opportunity to tell the story of William Tell.

ARCHIMEDE—Archimedes: In reference to his name say: 'Eureka! Give me a lever and I will lift the world.' There is also Archimedes' screw, but you are not expected to know what this is.

ARCHITECTES—Architects: All imbeciles. Always forget a house's staircase.

ARCHITECTURE: There are only four architectural orders. If, of course, you don't count the Egyptian, the Cyclopean, the Assyrian, the Indian, the Chinese, the Gothic, the Romanesque, etc.

ARGENT—Money: Cause of all evil. *Auri sacra fames*. The god of the day (don't confuse with Apollo). Ministers call it remuneration; lawyers, emoluments; doctors, fees; employees, salaries; workmen, pay; domestics, wages. Money doesn't make for happiness.

ARMEE—Army: The bastion of society.

ARSENIC: Can be found everywhere (recall Madame Lafarge). However, in some cultures it is eaten. [Marie Lafarge went to prison in 1840 for poisoning her husband, was pardoned in 1852 and assumed to be a victim of a miscarriage of justice]

ARTS: Will put you in hospital. What use is it since it can be replaced by machines which are better and quicker.

ARTISTES—Artists: All clowns. Praise their disinterestedness (*old-fashioned*). Be amazed that they are dressed like everyone else (*old-fashioned*). They earn crazy money, then throw it out of the window. Often invited to dine in town. A female artist can only be a prostitute. What they do cannot be called work.

ASPIC—Asp: Animal known thanks to Cleopatra's basket of figs.

ASSASSIN: Always cowardly, even when he is intrepid and audacious. Less reprehensible than an arsonist.

ASTRONOMIE—Astronomy: A beautiful science. Only useful to the navy. While on the subject, make fun of astrology.

ATHEE—Atheist: A nation of atheists would not be able to survive.

AUTEUR—Author: One should 'know writers'. Not necessary to know their names.

AUTRUCHE—Ostrich: Can digest rocks.

AVOCATS—Lawyers: There are too many lawyers in the House. Have bad judgement. Say of a lawyer who speaks badly: 'Yes, but he is good at law'.

B

BACCALAUREAT—Baccalaureate: Thunder against.

BADAUD—Idle gawper: All Parisians are show-offs, but then again nine out of ten are from the country. No one does any work in Paris.

BADIGEON (DANS LES EGLISES)—Whitewash (in churches): Thunder against. Artistic fury of this kind is extremely becoming.

BAGNOLET: Place famous for its blind people.

BAGUE—Ring: Very distinguished to wear one on the index finger. To put one on the thumb is too oriental. Wearing rings deforms the fingers.

BAILLEMENT—Yawn: One must say: 'Apologies. I'm not bored, it's my stomach.'

BALLONS—Balloons: With balloons we'll end up going to the moon. We are nowhere near being able to steer them.

BANDITS: Always ferocious.

BANQUET: Always permeated by the highest cordiality. One has the best memory of them, and never leaves without arranging a meeting for next year. A joker must say: 'At the banquet of life the ill-fated is a guest'. [Massenet, from *Stances/Adieux*]

BANQUIERS—Bankers: All rich. Arabs, sharks.

BARAGOUIN—Gobbledygook: What foreigners speak. Always laugh at a foreigner who speaks French badly.

BARBE—Beard: A sign of strength. Too much beard makes the hair fall out. Useful for protecting cravats.

BARBIER—Barber: Going to the '*frater*', to Figaro's. The barber of Louis XI. In the past used to bleed people. ['Frater', Lat. 'brother', was used even as late as Flaubert's day as a country term for barber]

BAS-BLEU—Bluestocking: Scornful term used to describe any

woman who is interested in intellectual matters. Quote Molière in support: 'When the capacity of her mind rises...' etc.

BASES DE LA SOCIETE—Pillars of society: That is property, family, religion, respect for the authorities. Defend them angrily if they are attacked.

BASILIQUE—Basilica: Pompous synonym for a church; is always imposing.

BASQUES—The Basques: The nation with the best runners.

BATON—Stick: More formidable than a sword.

BAUDRUCHE—Thin fleece made of cow or sheep's intestines: Only useful for making balloons/balls.

BAYADERES—Exotic dancer: A word to catch the imagination. All women from the East are *bayadères*.

BEETHOVEN: Don't pronounce it 'Bitovan'. Swoon whenever you hear one of his works.

BIBLE: The most ancient book in the world.

BIBLIOTHEQUE—Library: Always have one at home, particularly when one lives in the country.

BIERE—Beer: Avoid, it will give you a cold.

BILLIARD—Billiards: A noble game. Indispensable to country folk.

BLONDES: Hotter than brunettes (*see* Brunettes).

BOIS—Wood: Woods make one dream. Appropriate for writing poetry. In the autumn when taking a walk one should say: 'The leaves are falling...'

BONNET GREC—Smoking cap: Essential for the professional man. Lends his face an air of majesty.

BOUCHERS—Butchers: Terrifying during times of revolution.

BOUDDHISME—Buddhism: 'False religion of India'. (Bouillet dictionary definition, 1st edition) [Flaubert is mocking the error-ridden *Dictionnaire Universel de l'Histoire et de Géographie* by Nicolas Bouillet (1798-1864)]

BOUILLI (LE) — Broth:　Wholesome. Indistinguishable from the word soup: soup and broth.

BOSSUS — Hunchbacks:　Have enormous wit. Greatly sought after by oversexed women.

BOUDIN — Black pudding:　Sign of festivity in homes. Indispensable on Christmas Eve.

BOULET — Cannonball:　Tail wind from a cannon ball can blind one (death by asphyxiation).

BOURSE — Stock exchange:　Gauge of public opinion.

BOURSIERS — City traders:　All thieves.

BOUTONS — Pimples:　On the face or elsewhere, they are a sign of health and strong blood. Never try to squeeze them.

BRACONNIERS — Poachers:　All ex-convicts. Responsible for all crimes committed in the countryside. Should excite frenzied rage: 'No mercy sir, no mercy!'

BRAS — Arm:　To govern France one must be iron-fisted.

BRETELLES — Braces:　[Flaubert cannot support this entry]

BRETONS:　All nice people, but stubborn.

BRUNETTES:　Hotter than blondes (*see* Blondes).

BUDGET:　Never balanced.

BUFFON:　Used to put on oversleeves before writing. [The author of a forty-four volume *Histoire Naturelle*]

BUREAU — Office:　[Flaubert at a loss for words]

C

CAFE — Coffee:　Invigorating. Only good if it comes from Le Havre. At a large dinner party, should be taken standing up. Swallowing it without sugar is very chic: gives the impression that you've lived in the East.

CALVITIE — Baldness:　Always premature and caused by the

excesses of youth or by thinking great thoughts.

CAMPAGNE—The country: Country people always better than townsfolk: envy them. In the country all is forgiven: scruffy clothes, crude behaviour.

CANARDS—Ducks: They all come from Rouen.

CANONADE—Cannonade: Changes the weather.

CARABINS—Medical students: Sleep next to corpses. There are some who eat them.

CAREME—Lent: In essence no more than a hygiene measure.

CATAPLASME—Poultice: Must always be applied while waiting for the doctor to arrive.

CATHOLICISME—Catholicism: Has had a very favourable influence on the arts.

CAUCHEMAR—Nightmare: Comes from the stomach.

CAVALERIE—Cavalry: Nobler than the infantry.

CAVERNES—Caves: Usual dwelling place of thieves. Are always full of snakes.

CEDRE—Cedar: The one in the Botanical Gardens was brought back in a hat.

CELEBRITES (LES)—Celebrities: Dig into the slightest detail of their private life so that you can run them down.

CELIBATAIRES—Bachelors: All selfish and debauched. Should be taxed. Heading for a sad old age.

CENSURE—Censorship: Useful, whatever they may say.

CERCLE—Association: Always belong to one.

CERTIFICAT—Certificate: A guarantee for relatives and parents. Always a good thing.

CHALEUR—Heat: Always unbearable. Never drink when it is hot.

CHAMBRE-A-COUCHER—Bedroom: In an old castle: Henri IV will always have spent the night there.

CHAMEAU—Camel: Has two humps and the dromedary

just one. Or perhaps, the camel has one hump and the dromedary two (one doesn't know exactly; one gets muddled).

CHAMPAGNE: Sign of a grand dinner. Pretend to hate it and say that 'It's not really a wine'. Causes great enthusiasm among the lower classes. Russia consumes more of it than France. The means of spreading French ideas throughout Europe. During the Regency one did nothing but drink it. But one doesn't drink it, one 'pops' it open.

CHAMPIGNONS—Mushrooms: Should only be bought at the market. (Only eat those which come from the market.)

CHAPEAU—Hat: Complain about their shape.

CHARCUTIER—(Pork) butcher: Anecdote about pâté made from human flesh. *Charcutiers'* wives are all pretty.

CHARTREUX—Carthusian monks: Spend their time making Chartreuse, digging their graves and saying: 'Brother, in life we are in death.'

CHASSE—Hunting: Excellent exercise which one must pretend to love. Part of the splendour of royalty. The judiciary gets worked up about it.

CHAT—Cat: Cats are treacherous. Call them salon tigers. Cut off their tails to prevent vertigo.

CHATAIGNE—Chestnut: Female conker.

CHATEAU-FORT—Castle: Has always been laid siege to under Philippe Auguste.

CHEMINEE—Chimney: Always smokes. Subject of discussions relating to heating.

CHEMINS DE FER—Railways: If Napoleon had had them at his disposal, he would have been invincible. Go into ecstasies over this invention and say 'I, sir, the very same who speaking to you, was this morning at X; I left on the X train; I did my business there and at X o'clock I returned!'

CHEVAL—Horse: If it knew its own strength it wouldn't let itself be dominated. Horsemeat: Good subject for a pamphlet by a man who wants to present a serious image.

Racehorse: despise it. What use is it?

CHIEN—Dog: Specially designed for saving its master's life. Man's best friend.

CHIRURGIENS—Surgeons: Are tough-spirited: call them butchers.

CHOLERA: Melon gives you cholera. The cure is lots of tea with rum.

CHRISTIANISME—Christianity: Freed the slaves.

CIDRE—Cider: Ruins the teeth.

CIGARES—Cigars: Government monopoly cigars are 'all revolting'. The only good ones are smuggled.

CIRAGE—Shoe polish: Only good when you make it yourself.

CLAIR-OBSCUR—Chiaroscuro: No one knows what this is.

CLASSIQUES (LES)—Classics (The): One is supposed to know them.

CLOCHER—Steeple: The village one makes the heart beat faster.

CLOWN: His joints have been dislocated since childhood.

CLUB: Topic of irritation for conservatives. Confusion and argument about the pronunciation of the word.

COCHON—Pig: Since its insides are 'just like those of a human', it should be used in hospitals for teaching anatomy.

COCU—Cuckold: Every woman should do this.

COFFRES-FORTS—Safes: Very easy to work out their combinations.

COGNAC: Absolutely deadly. Excellent for certain illnesses. A good glass of cognac never does any harm. Kills intestinal worms if taken on an empty stomach.

COLLEGE, LYCEE: More prestigious than boarding school.

COLONIES (NOS)—Colonies (Our): Lament when they are mentioned.

COMEDIE—Comedy: In verse, this is no longer suited to our

times. One must, however, respect high comedy. *Castigat ridendo mores.*

COMETES — Comets: Make fun of people who used to be afraid of them.

COMMERCE — Business: Discuss which is more noble: business or industry.

COMMUNION: First communion: the most wonderful day of one's life.

CONCUPISCENCE — Lust: Priest's word to describe carnal desire.

CONFISEURS — Confectioners: All inhabitants of Rouen are confectioners.

CONFORTABLE — Comfortable: A precious modern discovery.

CONSERVATOIRE: It is imperative to subscribe to the Conservatoire.

CONSTIPATION: All literary people are constipated. Affects political convictions.

CONVERSATION: Politics and religion should be avoided.

COPAHU — Copaiba oil: Pretend not to know what it's used for. [A stimulant and occasional diuretic]

COR (AUX PIEDS) — Corn (on the foot): Indicate changing weather conditions better than a barometer. Very dangerous when they are cut out badly; give some examples of dreadful accidents.

COR (DE CHASSE) — Horn (hunting): Impressive in woods (and in the evening on water).

CORDE — Rope: People don't realise how strong rope is. It is stronger than iron.

CORPS — Body: If we realised how our bodies are put together we would not dare to move.

CORSET: Prevents one from having children.

COSAQUES — Cossacks: Eat candles.

COTON—Cotton wool: Especially useful for putting in ears. One of the pillars of society in the Lower Seine region.

COURTISANE (sic)—High-class prostitute: A necessary evil. Safeguard of our daughters and sisters while there are bachelors about. However, they should be harried without mercy. One can no longer go out with one's wife because of their presence on the streets. Always working girls seduced by rich bourgeois.

CRAPAUD—Toad: Male frog. Has very dangerous venom. Lives inside stones.

CREOLE: Lives in a hammock.

CRITIQUE—Critic: Always eminent. Supposed to know everything and everyone, to have read and seen everything. When one annoys you call him an Aristarchus (or eunuch).
[Aristarchus was the first to say the earth revolved around the sun]

CROCODILE: Imitates children's cries in order to attract people.

CROISADES—Crusades: Were beneficial for Venetian trade.

CRUCIFIX: Looks good in an alcove and by the guillotine.

CUISINE—Cooking: In restaurants: always makes you feel ill. The wife's: always wholesome. In the south: too spicy or too much oil.

CUJAS: Inseparable from Bartholde; one doesn't know who wrote what, it doesn't matter. Say to anyone studying the law 'You are immersed in Cujas and Bartholde'. [French lawyers]

CYGNE—Swan: Sings before dying. Can break a man's thigh-bone with its wing. The swan of Cambrai was not a bird but a man (a bishop) called Fénelon. The swan of Mantua is Virgil. The swan of Pesaro is Rossini.

CYPRES—Cypress: Only grows in cemeteries.

D

DAGUERROTYPE: Will replace painting.

DAMAS—Damascus: The only place where they know how to make sabres. All good blades are from Damascus.

DAUPHIN—Dolphin: Carries children on its back.

DEBAUCHE—Debauchery: Cause of all bachelors' illnesses.

DECOR DE THEATRE—Stage scenery: This is not painting: they throw a bucket of colours haphazardly onto a backdrop, then spread them around with a broom. In the distance the lights will produce the desired illusion.

DECORATION DE LA LEGION D'HONNEUR: Make fun of it but covet it. When you get it always say you didn't ask for it.

DECORUM: Gives one prestige. Seizes the imagination of the masses. 'It is essential! Essential!'

DEFAITE—Defeat: Suffer one and it's so complete that there is no one left to bring news of it.

DEICIDE: Express indignation against, although it is not a frequently committed crime.

DEJEUNER-DES-GARÇONS—Boys' night out: Demand oysters, white wine and womanizing.

DEMELOIR—Wide-toothed comb: Makes the hair fall out.

DEMOSTHENE—Demosthenes: Never gave a speech without a pebble in the mouth.

DENTS—Teeth: Spoiled by cider, tobacco, sugared almonds, ice cream, sleeping with the mouth open and drinking immediately after soup.

DENT-OEILLIERE—Eye-tooth: Dangerous to have them pulled out because they are connected to the eyes. Pulling out a tooth 'is no fun'.

DEPURATIF—Depurative: Take it on the sly.

DEPUTE—Deputy: To be one is the highest honour. Thunder against the Chamber of Deputies. Too many blabbermouths in the Chamber. They don't do anything.

DESCARTES: *Cogito, ergo sum.*

DESERT: Produces dates.

DESSERT: Express regret that one doesn't sing during it. Virtuous people despise it. 'Absolutely not. No cakes! I never have dessert!'

DESSIN (L'ART DU) — Drawing (the art of): Composed of three things: line, shading and fine stippling. There is also the masterstroke. But the masterstroke can be performed only by the expert (Christophe). [The reference is presumably to Joseph Christophe (1664-1748) author of a vast history painting at Versailles]

DEVOIRS — Duties: Demand them from others, free oneself of them. Others have duties to us, but we don't have duties to them.

DEVOUEMENT — Devotion: Complain that others lack it. 'We are entirely inferior to the dog in this respect.'

DIAMANT — Diamond: We will eventually be able to manufacture them! And think that it's nothing more than coal! If we were to find one in its natural state we wouldn't pick it up!

DICTIONNAIRE — Dictionary: Say: only made for ignoramuses.

DICTIONNAIRE DES RIMES — Rhyming dictionary: Use one of those? Never!

DIDEROT: Always followed by d'Alembert.

DIEU — God: Voltaire himself said: 'If God did not exist, we should have invented him.'

DILETTANTE: Rich man who subscribes to the opera.

DILIGENCES — Stagecoach: Regret the passing of the age of the stagecoach.

DINER — Dinner: In the past one dined at midday, now one dines at impossible hours. Our fathers' dinner was our lunch, and our lunch was their dinner. Dining so late cannot be called dinner, but also supper.

DIOGENE — Diogenes: 'I am seeking a human.' 'Stop blocking my sun.'

DIPLOMATIE — Diplomacy: Wonderful career (but bristling

with trouble and full of riddles). Only suitable for nobles. Profession of rather vague significance, but superior to commerce. A diplomat is always refined and penetrating.

DIPLOME — Diploma: Sign of learning. Proves nothing.

DIRECTOIRE (LE) — Directory (the):   The shame of the Directory. 'In those days honour had taken refuge with the army. In Paris, women went about completely naked.' [French revolutionary government]

DISSECTION: An outrage to the dignity of death.

DIVORCE: If Napoleon hadn't divorced he would still be on the throne.

DIX (LE CONSEIL DES) — Ten (Council of):   Nobody knows what it was, but it was terrifying. Wore masks during sessions. Be frightened of it even today.

DJINN: Name of an oriental dance.

DOCTEUR — Doctor: Always preceded by 'good', and among men in informal conversation, by damned: 'Ah! Damn it, the doctor!' All materialists. 'You won't find God at the end of a scalpel'.

DOCTRINAIRES;   Despise them. Why? One has no idea.

DOGE: Married the sea. Only one is known: Marino Faliero.

DOLMEN: Has to do with the Gauls. Stone used for druid sacrifices. Only found in Brittany. Nothing else is known about it.

DOME: Architectural *tour de form* (sic). Be amazed that it can stay up. Give two examples: Les Invalides and St Peter's in Rome.

DOMINOS — Dominoes: One plays this much better when one is tipsy.

DOMPTEURS DE BETES FEROCES — Tamers of wild animals: Use obscene methods.

DONJON: Stir up gloomy ideas.

DORMIR — Sleeping: Sleeping too much thickens the blood.

DORTOIRS—Dormitories: Always spacious and well-aired. For the moral benefit of pupils, they are preferable to bedrooms.

DOS—Back: A slap on the back can give one tuberculosis.

DOUANE—Customs: One must revolt against them and defraud them.

DOULEUR—Grief: Always has a positive outcome. Genuine pain is always subdued.

DOUTE—Doubt: Worse than negation.

DRAPEAU NATIONAL—National flag: Makes the heart beat faster.

DROIT (LE)—Law (The): No one knows what this is.

DUEL: Thunder against. Is not a proof of courage. The prestige of a man who has fought a duel.

DUPE: Better to be a rogue than a dupe.

E

EAU—Water: The water in Paris gives you colic. Sea water holds you up when swimming. The water in Cologne smells good.

ECHAFAUD—Scaffold: On mounting it, prepare oneself to say a few eloquent words before dying.

ECHARPE—Sash: Poetic.

ECHECS (JEU DES)—Chess: Reproduces military tactics. All great army commanders were good at it. Too serious for a game, too pointless for a science.

ECHO: Give the examples of the Pantheon and the Pont de Neuilly.

ECLECTICISME—Eclecticism: Thunder against, since this is an immoral philosophy.

ECOLES—Schools: The Polytechnic is what all mothers

dream of (*old-fashioned*). The terror of the bourgeois during the riots when he learns that the Polytechnic sympathises with the workers (*old-fashioned*). Simply saying 'the School' gives the impression that one has been there. At Saint-Cyr: young noblemen. At the school of medicine: all fanatics. At the school of law: young men of good family.

ECONOMIE — Economy: Always preceded by 'order', leads to fortune. Tell the story of Laffitte picking up a pin in the yard of the banker Perrégaux.

ECONOMIE POLITIQUE — Political economy: Unfeeling science.

ECRIT, BIEN ECRIT — Written, well written: Porters' term for describing the newspaper serials which amuse them.

ECRITURE — Handwriting: Beautiful handwriting will get you everywhere. Indecipherable: a sign of science, for example, doctors' prescriptions.

EGOISME — Egotism: Complain about it in other people and do not notice it in oneself.

ELEPHANTS: Distinguished by their memories and love the sun.

EMAIL — Enamel: Its secret is lost.

EMBONPOINT — Stoutness: Sign of wealth and laziness.

EMIGRES — Emigrés: Earn their living by giving guitar lessons and making salad.

EMIR: Only said in reference to Abd-el-Kader. [Emir of Mascara, a nineteenth-century Arab leader imprisoned and later freed by Napoleon III]

ENCEINTE — Enclosure: Goes well in official speeches: 'Gentlemen, between these four walls'.

ENCRIER — Inkwell: Give as a present to a doctor.

ENCYCLOPEDIE — Diderot's Encyclopédie: Laugh at it pityingly as at a piece of rococo work and even thunder against.

ENFANTS — Children: Affect a lyrical tenderness towards them when there are other people around.

ENGELURE—Chilblain: Sign of good health. Caused by warming up when one had been cold.

ENTERREMENT—Funeral: Say of the deceased: 'And to think I had dinner with him only a week ago!'

ENTHOUSIASME—Enthusiasm: Can only be inspired by the return of the Emperor's ashes.

ENTR'ACTE—Interval: Always too long.

ENVERGURE—Wingspan: Argue about the pronunciation of the word.

EPACTE, NOMBRE D'OR, LETTRE DOMINICALE—Epact, Golden Numbers, Sunday letters: On calendars. One doesn't know what they are.

EPARGNE (CAISSE D')—Savings bank: Opportunity for domestic servants to steal.

EPEE—Sword: Regret that the times when one could wear one have passed.

EPERONS—Spurs: Look good on a pair of boots.

EPICURE—Epicurist: Despise him.

EPUISEMENT—Exhaustion: Always premature.

EPOQUE (LA NOTRE)—Our epoch: Thunder against. Complain that it's not poetic. Call it the epoch of compromise, of decadence.

EQUITATION—Riding: Good exercise for slimming. Example: all cavalry soldiers are thin. For putting on weight. Example: all cavalry officers have large stomachs.

ERECTION: Only said of monuments.

ERUDITION—Erudition: Scorn it as the mark of a narrow mind.

ESCRIME—Fencing: Fencing masters know artful thrusts.

ESCROC—Crook: Always a man of society.

ESPLANADE—Esplanade: Only found near Les Invalides.

ESTOMAC—Stomach: All illnesses come from the stomach.

ETAGERE—Rack: Essential for pretty women.

ETERNUEMENT—Sneeze: After someone says: God bless you, enter into a discussion on the origins of this expression.

ETOILE—Star: Everyone follows his own.

ETRENNES—Christmas presents: Express indignation.

ETALON—Stallion: Always fierce. A woman ought to ignore the difference between a stallion and a horse.

ETE—Summer: Always exceptional.

ETRANGER—Abroad: A taste for everything that comes from abroad is proof of a liberal mind. Running down everything which is not French is proof of patriotism.

ETRUSQUE—Etruscan: All old vases are Etruscan.

ETYMOLOGIE—Etymology: Nothing is easier to find with Latin and a little thought.

EUNUQUE—Eunuch: Fulminate against the castrato singers of the Sistine Chapel.

EXECUTIONS CAPITALES—Public executions: Complain about women who go to watch them.

EXERCICE—Exercise: Protects against all illnesses: always advise it.

EXPOSITION—Exhibition: Subject of delirious excitement in the nineteenth century.

EXTIRPER—Extirpate: This verb is only used in reference to heresies and corns.

F

FABRIQUE—Factory: Dangerous neighbourhood.

FACTURE—Bill: Always too much.

FAISCEAUX—Stack of arms: Making one is the most taxing thing they do in the National Guard.

FARD—Make-up: Damages the skin.

FAISAN — Pheasant: Very chic for dinner.

FAUBOURGS — Suburbs: Scary during revolutions.

FAUX RATELLIER — False teeth: Third set of teeth. Beware of swallowing them in your sleep.

FAUX MONNAYEURS — Counterfeiters: Always work underground.

FAUTE — Mistake: 'What is worse than a crime is a mistake' (Talleyrand). 'There are no more mistakes for you to make' (Thiers). These two phrases should be pronounced very weightily.

FEMME — Woman: [On this occasion Flaubert has nothing to say on the subject]

FEODALITE — Feudalism: Have no exact understanding of what this is, but thunder against it.

FEUILLETONS — Serials: Cause of subversion of morals. Argue about the probable outcome. Write to the author to give him ideas.

FEMMES DE CHAMBRE — Chambermaids: Prettier than their mistresses. Know all their secrets and betray them. Always deflowered by the son of the household.

FERMIERS — Farmers: All comfortably off.

FEU — Fire: Purifies everything. When one hears the cry 'Fire!' one begins by losing one's head.

FIEVRE — Fever: Sign of the strength of the blood. Caused by prunes.

FIGARO (LE MARIAGE DE) — The Marriage of Figaro: Another cause of the Revolution.

FILLES — Girls: Young girls: they should avoid all kinds of books. Pronounce the word hesitantly.

FLAMANT — Flamingo: The bird is thus named because it comes from Flanders. [Identical word in French]

FOETUS — Foetus: Any anatomical specimen preserved in alcohol.

FONCTIONNAIRE—Civil servant: Inspires respect whatever his job is.

FONDEMENT—Foundation: The news never has any.

FONDS SECRETS—Secret funds: Incalculable sums with which ministers buy consciences. Express indignation against.

FORCATS—Convicts: Always sinister-looking. All very good with their hands. There are men of genius doing hard labour.

FORNARINA: This was a beautiful woman. No point in knowing any more about her. [The portrait of Raphael's mistress, circa 1509, is in the Barberini Gallery, Rome]

FORTUNE: When someone tells you about a large fortune don't forget to say: 'Yes but is it quite secure?'

FOSSILES—Fossils: Proof of the flood. A joke in good taste when talking about an academic.

FOUDRE DU VATICAN—Wrath of the Vatican: Laugh at it.

FOULE—Crowd: Always has the right instinct.

FOURMIS—Ants: A good example to mention in the presence of a spendthrift. They gave us the idea of savings banks. [Reference to a fable of La Fontaine]

FOULARD—Scarf: It is genteel to blow one's nose into one.

FOURRURE—Fur coat: Sign of wealth.

FOUTRE—Damned: Use this only as a swear-word, if at all.

FRANÇAIS—The French: The leading nation in the universe.

FRANC-MAÇONNERIE—Freemasonry: Another cause of the Revolution! The initiation ceremony is frightening: some people die during it! Cause of household disputes. Clerics take a dim view of it. What can be its great secret?

FRANCS-TIREURS—Irregulars: More terrible than the enemy.

FRESQUE—Frescos: No longer made.

FRICASSEE: Only good in the country.

FRISER, FRISURE—Curls: Do not suit men.

FROID—Cold: Healthier than heat.

FROMAGE—Cheese: State Brillat-Savarin's principle: 'a dinner without cheese is like a beauty with a missing eye'.

FRONT—Forehead: Wide and bald, sign of genius.

FRONTISPIECE—Frontispiece: Great men look good on them.

FRUSTE—Worn: Everything which is antique is worn and everything which is worn is antique. A good thing to remember when buying curiosities.

FUGUE—Fugue: One does not know what they consist of but one must assert that they are difficult and very boring.

FULMINER—Fulminate: A good verb.

FUSIL—Rifle: Always have one of them in the countryside.

FUSILLER—Firing squad: Nobler than the guillotine. Joy of the individual who is granted this favour.

FUSION DES BRANCHES ROYALES—Merging of all the branches of the royal family: Hope for it, at all times!

G

GAGNE-PETIT—Low-wage earner: A good sign for a boutique, to inspire confidence.

GALBE—Curves: In front of every statue which you look at say: that has some lovely curves.

GALETS—Pebbles: Must be brought back from the seaside.

GAMIN—Urchin: Always preceded by 'Paris'. Invariably has lots of spirit.

GARES DE CHEMIN DE FER—Railway stations: Go into ecstasies in front of them and pronounce them models of architectural achievement.

GARNISON DE JEUNE HOMME: Garrison of young men. *Id est culex pubensis.*

GAUCHERS—Left-handed people: Terrifying when fencing. More dexterous than those who use the right hand.

GENDARMES—Policemen: Bastions of society.

GENERATION SPONTANEE—Spontaneous generation: Socialist idea. [Related to uprisings]

GENOVEFAIN: One does not know what this is.

GENTILHOMME—Gentleman: They no longer exist.

GENIE (LE)—Genius: No point admiring it, it's a neurosis.

GENRE EPISTOLAIRE—Epistolary style: A genre exclusively reserved for women.

GIAOUR: Fierce expression of unknown significance, but one knows it has to do with the East.

GIBERNE—Cartridge pouch: Holster for the baton of the Marshal of France. [Napoleon said every humble soldier symbolically carried a marshal's baton in his cartridge pouch]

GIBELOTTE—Rabbit stew: Always made with cat.

GIBIER—Game: Only high game is good.

GIRONDINS—Girondists: Deserve more sympathy than blame.

GLACES—Ice cream: Dangerous to eat.

GLEBE (LA)—Soil: Be sorry for the state of the…

GLOIRE—Glory: Is nothing but a puff of smoke.

GOBELINS (TAPISSERIE DES): An incredible masterpiece which takes fifty years to complete. Standing in front of it, cry: 'This is more beautiful than painting!' The tapestry-worker does not know what he's making.

GOD SAVE THE KING: In Béranger is pronounced: God savé the King. Rhymes with Sauvé, préservé…

GOMME ELASTIQUE—Rubber: Made from a horse's scrotum.

GOTHIQUE—Gothic: Style of architecture which brings more to religion than others.

GRAMMAIRE—Grammar: Teach it to children from the earliest possible age as if it was something clear and easy.

GRAS—Fat: Fat people do not need to learn to swim. They are the despair of executioners because of the difficulties they present. Example: la Du Barry. [The Comtesse du Barry was so fat at the time of her execution in 1793 that the guillotine at first refused to do its work]

GRELE—Pockmarked: All pockmarked women are oversexed.

GRENIER—Loft: It's great up there when you're twenty!

GRENOUILLE—Frog: Female toad.

GROG: Not a genteel drink.

GROTTES A STALACTITES—Cave with stalactites: There has been a famous party, ball or supper inside, given by an important person. One sees something there 'similar to organ pipes'. Mass was said there during the Revolution.

GROUPE—Group: Looks good on a mantelpiece or in politics.

GUERILLA: Does more harm to the enemy than the regular army.

GULF-STREAM: Famous Norwegian town, recently discovered. [A popular misconception of the new oceanographic research]

GYMNASTIQUE—Gymnastics: Impossible to do too much of them. Exhausting for children.

GYMNASE—Theatre: Branch of the Comédie-Francaise.

H

HABIT NOIR—Black clothes: In the provinces these are the last word in ceremony and inconvenience.

HALEINE—Breath: To have 'bad' breath gives one a 'distinguished air'.

HAMAC—Hammock: Characteristic to the Creoles. Indispensable in a garden. Persuade oneself that a hammock is more comfortable than a bed.

HAMEAU—Hamlet: A touching word. Good in poetry.

HANNETONS—May-bug: Good subject for a pamphlet. Their complete destruction is the dream of every prefect.

HAQUENEE—Palfrey: White animal of the Middle Ages, now extinct.

HARAS (LA QUESTION DES)—The matter of the stud farm: Good subject for parliamentary discussion.

HARENG—Herring: The wealth of Holland.

HARPE—Harp: Shows off to advantage the arms and hands. In carvings is only played on ruins. Produces heavenly harmonies.

HEBREU—Hebrew: Everything that one doesn't understand.

HEIDUQUE—Haiduk: Confuse with eunuch.

HELICE—Propeller: The future of mechanics.

HEMICYCLE—Semicircle: Only that of the Beaux Arts is worth knowing. [The mural in the theatre of the Ecole des Beaux Arts by Paul Delaroche (1797-1856) which shows the greatest artists and architects in the company of the Muses]

HEMORROIDES—Haemorrhoids: Caused by sitting on stoves and stone benches.

HENRI III et HENRI IV: When talking about these kings don't forget to cry out: 'All the Henris were unfortunate!'

HERMAPHRODITE: Arouses curiosity. Try to see one of them.

HERNIE—Hernia: Everyone has one of them without knowing it.

HIATUS: Not to be tolerated.

HIEROGLYPHES—Hieroglyphics: Ancient language of the Egyptians, invented by priests to hide their illicit secrets. 'And to think that there are people who can understand them!' 'Perhaps they're having us on after all?'

HIPPOCRATE—Hippocrates: He must always be quoted in Latin because he wrote in Greek.

HIVER—Winter: Always exceptional (see Summer). Healthier than other seasons.

HOBERAUX DE CAMPAGNE—Country squire: Have the highest contempt for them.

HOMERE—Homer: Never existed. Famous for his way of laughing: a Homeric laugh.

HORIZONS—Horizons: Find natural ones beautiful and political ones dismal.

HOSPODAR: Goes well in a sentence concerning 'the Eastern question'.

HOTELS: Only good in Switzerland.

HUGO (VICTOR): Was very wrong to get involved in politics.

HUILE D'OLIVE—Olive oil: Never good. One must have a friend in Marseilles who sends you little casks.

HUITRES—Oysters: One no longer eats them! They are too expensive!

HUMEUR—Secretions: Rejoice when they come out and be amazed that the human body can hold such large quantities of them.

HUMIDITE—Humidity: Cause of all illnesses.

HYDRE (DE L'ANARCHIE)—The Hydra of anarchy: Try to conquer it.

HYDROTHERAPIE—Hydrotherapy: Cures all illnesses and causes them.

HYPOTHEQUE—Mortgage: Demand 'the reform of the mortgage system', very chic.

HYSTERIA: Confuse it with nymphomania.

I

IDEAL: Completely useless.

IDEOLOGUE: All journalists are ideologues.

IDOLATRES — Idolaters: Are cannibals.

ILLISIBLE — Illegible: A doctor's prescription must be illegible, all signatures, ditto.

ILLUSIONS: Pretend to have lots. Grumble about losing them.

ILOTES — Helots: An example for your son, but one does not know where to find them.

IMAGES: There are always too many in poetry.

IMAGINATION: Always lively. Be wary of your own. And run down other people's.

IMBECILLES — Imbeciles: Those who don't think as we do.

IMBROGLIO: The root of all theatrical works.

IMPERATRICES — Empresses: All beautiful.

IMPERIALISTES — Imperialists: All honest, peaceful, polite and distinguished people.

IMPERMEABLE — Raincoat: A very flattering piece of clothing. Dangerous because it impedes perspiration.

IMPIE — The Impious: Thunder against.

IMPORTATION — Imports: Worm eating away at trade.

IMPRIMERIE — Printing works: Marvellous invention. Has done more harm than good.

INAUGURATION: Subject of joy.

INCENDIE — Fire: A sight to see.

INCOGNITO: The dress of princes on their travels.

INDOLENCE: A consequence of hot countries.

INFANTICIDE: Only committed by the masses.

INFINITESIMAL: One doesn't know what this is but it is related to homeopathy.

INGENIEUR—Engineer: First choice of career for a young man. Knows all the sciences.

INHUMATION—Burial: Too often premature: tell stories of corpses which ate their own arms to satisfy their hunger.

INNEES (IDEES)—Innate ideas: Poke fun at.

INNOCENCE: Proved by impassivity.

INNOVATION: Always dangerous.

INONDIES—Flood victims: Always from the Loire area.

INQUISITION: Its crimes have been seriously exaggerated.

INSCRIPTION: Always cuneiform.

INSPIRATION (POÉTIQUE):   Provoked by: the view of the sea, love, women etc.

INSTITUT (L')—The Institute of France: The members of the Institute are all old men and wear green taffeta visors.

INSTITUTRICES—Governesses: Always from excellent families which have fallen upon hard times. Dangerous at home: corrupt the husband.

INSTRUCTION—Education: Let it be known that you have had a great deal of it. The masses have no need for it to earn a living.

INTEGRITE—Integrity: Belongs above all to the judiciary.

INTRIGUE: The way to everything.

INTRODUCTION: Obscene word.

INVENTEURS—Inventors: Always die in hospital. Someone else profits from their discoveries; this is not fair.

ITALIE—Italy: Should be visited immediately after the wedding. Very disappointing; is not as beautiful as they say.

ITALIENS—Italians: All musicians, treacherous.

IVOIRE—Ivory: Only use when referring to teeth.

J

JALOUSIE — Jealousy: Terrible passion.

JAMBAGE — A leg-over, or droit de seigneur: Do not believe in it.

JAMBON — Ham: Always from Mainz. But beware of trichinosis.

JANSENISM: One does not know what this is but it is very chic to talk about it.

JARDINS ANGLAIS — English Gardens: More natural than gardens in the French style.

JARNAC (COUP DE) — Stab in the back: Express indignation against this, which in the main was completely loyal. [The Comte de Jarnac won a celebrated duel in 1547 with an inadvertent stroke]

JAVELOT — Javelin: As good as a rifle when you know how to use one.

JEU — Games: Express indignation at this fatal passion.

JESUITES — Jesuits: Have a hand in all revolutions. One has no idea how numerous they are. Never mention 'the battle of the Jesuits'.

JEUNE HOMME — Young man: Always a wag. He has to be. Be amazed if he isn't.

JOCKEY: Deplore the species.

JOCKEY CLUB: Its members are all young wags and very rich. Simply saying 'the Jockey' is very chic and gives the impression that one is a member.

JOUETS — Toys: Should always be scientific.

JOUISSANCE — Delight, but also 'coming':   Obscene word.

JOURNAUX — Newspapers: Can't get by without them. But thunder against.

JUJUBE—Jojoba: One has no idea what it's made from.

JUSTICE: Never worry about it.

K

KEEPSAKE: Should be located on the table in the sitting room.

KIOSQUE—Kiosk: Place in a park where you can find tasty things.

KNOUT: Word which annoys the Russians.

KORAN: Book of Mohammed which is all about women.

L

LABORATOIRE—Laboratory: One should have one at one's country place.

LABOUREUR—Ploughmen: Where would we be without them?

LAC—Lake: Have a woman with you when you sail on one.

LACONISME—Terseness: Language which you don't speak.

LACUSTRES (LES VILLES)—Lakeside towns: Deny their existence because it's not possible to live under water.

LAGUNE—Lagoon: A town on the Adriatic.

LAIT—Milk: Dissolves oysters. Attracts snakes. Whitens the skin; women in Paris bathe in milk every morning.

LANCETTE—Lancet: Always have one in your pocket but be cautious about using it.

LANGOUSTE—Crayfish: Female lobster.

LANGUES VIVANTES—Modern languages; France's

troubles arise from the fact that we don't know enough of them.

LATIN: Man's natural language. Spoils handwriting. Only useful for reading the inscriptions on public fountains. Be suspicious of quotations in Latin: they are always hiding something risqué.

LETHARGIE—Lethargy: Sometimes it lasts for years.

LIBELLE—Lampoon: No longer done.

LIBERTE—Liberty: Liberty! What crimes are committed in your name! We have all the necessary ones.

LIBERTINAGE—Licentiousness: Only exists in large towns.

LIBRE ECHANGE—Free trade: Cause of all the ills and sufferings of business.

LIEVRE—Hare: Sleeps with its eyes open.

LIGUEURS—Members of the League: Vanguard of liberalism in France. [Group of Catholics who opposed the Calvinists]

LION: Generous. Always plays with a ball.

LILAS—Lilac: Brings pleasure because it announces the arrival of summer.

LINGES—Linen: One must never show too much of it, never enough.

LITTERATURE—Literature: Occupation of idlers.

LITTRE: Snigger when you hear his name: 'The man who says that we are descended from monkeys!' [Littré 1801-1881, author of the *Dictionnaire de la langue française*]

LIVRE—Book: Whichever it is, it is always too long.

LORD: Rich Englishman.

LORGNON—Lorgnette: Insolent and distinguished.

LUNE—Moon: Inspires melancholy. Perhaps it is inhabited?

LUXE—Luxury: The downfall of states.

LYNX: Animal famous for its eye.

M

MACADAM—Tarmac: Has done away with revolutions. There is no longer any way of constructing barricades. Nevertheless, is very inconvenient.

MACHIAVELLIAN: One should not say this word without trembling.

MACHIAVELLI: One should not have read him, but should view him as a blackguard.

MAESTRO: Italian word meaning pianist.

MAGIE—Magic: Make fun of it.

MAGISTRATURE—Public office: Good career for a young man. All pederasts.

MAGNETISME—Magnetism: Nice subject of conversation and useful for flirting with the ladies.

MAIRE DE VILLAGE—Small town mayor: Always ridiculous.

MAJOR: Nowadays can only be found in hotel dining rooms.

MAL DE MER—Seasickness: To avoid experiencing it, it is sufficient to think about something else.

MALADE—Ill person: To lift the spirits of someone who is ill, laugh at his ailment and deny that he is suffering.

MALADIE DES NERFS—Nervous illness: Always posturing.

MALEDICTION: Always given by a father.

MALTHUS: 'The infamous Malthus.'

MAMELUCKS—Mamelukes: Ancient people of the East (Egypt).

MANDOLINE—Mandolin: Essential for seducing Spaniards.

MARSEILLAIS—The people of Marseilles: All witty.

MARTYRS: All the first Christians were martyrs.

MASQUE—Mask: Makes one witty.

MATELAS—Mattress: The harder, the more hygienic.

MATHEMATIQUE—Mathematics: Toughens the heart.

MATINAL—Early rising: Proof of morality. If one goes to bed at four in the morning and gets up at eight, one is lazy, but if one goes to bed at nine in the evening in order to get up the next day at five, one is active.

MAZARINADES—Songs against Cardinal Mazarin: Be suspicious of them, it's useless to know a single one. [Cardinal Richelieu's successor]

MECANIQUE—Mechanics: Inferior part of mathematics.

MEDAILLE—Medal: Only made in antiquity.

MEDICINE: Mock it when one is in good health.

MELANCOLIE—Melancholy: Sign of a distinguished heart and an elevated spirit.

MELODRAMES—Melodramas: Less immoral than dramas.

MELON: Nice subject of dinner-table conversation. Is it a vegetable? Is it a fruit? The English, amazingly, eat it for dessert.

MEMOIRE—Memory: Grumble about one's own and even boast that you don't have one. But blush if someone says you are lacking in judgement.

MENAGE—Domesticity: Always speak of it with respect.

MENDICITE—Mendacity: Should be forbidden but never is.

MER—Sea: Has no bottom. Image of the infinite. Gives rise to great thoughts.

MERCURE—Mercury: Kills illnesses and ill people.

MERIDIONAUX—Southerners: All poets.

MESSAGE: Nobler than a letter.

METALLURGIE—Metallurgy: Very chic. [Flaubert is referring to the curiosity that in pre-revolutionary France iron-foundry was the sole industrial activity allowed to the aristocracy]

METAMORPHOSE—Metamorphosis: Laugh at the times when people believed in it. Ovid invented it.

METAPHORES—Metaphors: Writing style is always too full of them.

METAPHYSIQUE—Metaphysics: Laugh at it: gives the impression of a superior mind.

METHODE—Method: Useless.

MIDI (CUISINE DU)—Mediterranean cooking: Always made with garlic. Thunder against.

MINISTRE—Minister: The last word in human glory.

MINUIT—Midnight: The limit of happiness and honest pleasures; everything that one does after that is immoral.

MISSIONAIRES—Missionaries: All eaten or crucified.

MOBILIER—Furniture: Always worry about yours.

MONTRE—Watch: Only good if it comes from Geneva. In pantomimes, when someone pulls out his watch, it must be an onion. This joke never fails.

MOSAIQUES—Mosaics: The secret of them is lost.

MONSTRES—Monsters: One no longer sees them.

MOUCHARDS—Informers: All belong to the police.

MOULIN—Windmill: Looks nice in a landscape.

MOUSTIQUE—Mosquito: More dangerous than any wild animal.

MOUTARDE—Mustard: Ruins the stomach.

MUSEE—Museum: Of Versailles: revisits the great achievements of natural glory. A good idea of King Louis-Philippe. The Louvre: should be avoided by young girls. Dupuytren: very useful for showing to young men. [The Musuem of Baron Dupuytren (1777-1835) contained interesting anatomical specimens]

MUSICIEN—Musician: The characteristic of a true musician

is to compose no music, to play not a single instrument and to despise virtuosos.

MUSIQUE — Music: Makes one think of many things. Has a soothing effect on behaviour e.g. la Marseillaise.

N

NATIONS — Nations: Reunite all races.

NAVIRE — Ships: Good ones are only made in Bayonne.

NECTAR: Confuse it with ambrosia.

NEGRES — Negroes: Be amazed that their saliva is white and that they speak French.

NEGRESSES — Negresses: Hotter than white women (*see* Brunettes and Blondes).

NEOLOGISME — Neologism: The plague of the French language.

NERVEUX — Nervous: Is said whenever one cannot understand an illness; this explanation will satisfy the listener.

NOBLESSE — Nobility: Despise it and envy it.

NOEUD GORDIEN — Gordian Knot: Has to do with antiquity.

NORMANDS — Normans: Believe that they say 'Haaversaack' and make fun of their cotton bonnets.

NOTAIRES — Solicitors: Not to be trusted these days.

NUMISMATIQUE — Numismatics: Has to do with the high sciences, inspires immense respect.

O

OASIS — Oasis: An inn in the desert.

OBUS—Artillery shell: Useful for making pendulums and inkwells.

OCTROI—City tolls: One must evade them.

ODEON: Make jokes about how far away it is.

ODEUR—Smell (of feet): A sign of good health.

OEUF—Egg: Starting point for a philosophical essay on the origin of life.

OFFENBACH: As soon as one hears his name one must hold together two fingers of the right hand to keep oneself safe from the evil eye. Very Parisian, very fashionable.

OISEAU—Bird: To wish to be one and to say, sighing: 'Wings! Wings!' is the sign of a poetic soul.

OMEGA—Omega: Second letter of the Greek alphabet, since one always says alpha and omega.

OMNIBUS: One can never find a seat. Invented by Louis XIV. 'I, sir, have seen tricycles which have only three wheels!' [Les Tricycles was a Paris bus company of the early nineteenth century aimed at avoiding the tax on four-wheelers]

OPERA (COULISSES DE L')—Backstage: Mohammed's heaven on earth. [A reference to the supposed looseness of chorus girls]

OPTIMIST: Equivalent of imbecile.

ORAISON—Orison: All of Bossuet's speeches.

ORCHESTRE—Orchestra: Image of society: everyone has their role and there is a leader.

ORCHITE—Orchitis: Man's disease. [Inflammation of the testicle]

ORDRE (L')—Order: What crimes one commits in your name!

OREILLER—Pillow: Never use one, it makes you hunchbacked.

ORGUE—Organ: Lifts the soul towards God.

ORIENTALISTE—Orientalist: A man who has travelled a lot.

ORIGINAL—Unusual: Laugh at everything which is original. Detest it, scorn it, and eradicate it if one can.

ORTHOGRAPHIE—Orthography: Believe in it as one believes in mathematics (in geometry).

OUVRIER—Worker: Always honest when he isn't rioting.

OURS—Bear: Usually called 'Martin'. Tell the story of the invalid who on seeing a watch fall into the pit, climbed down into it and was devoured.

P

PAGANINI: Never tuned his violin. Famous for the length of his fingers.

PAIN—Bread: One does not know what impurities there are in bread.

PALLADIUM: Ancient fortress.

PALMIER—Palm tree: Gives local colour.

PALMYRE—Palmyra: A queen of Egypt? Ruins? One doesn't know.

PARADOXE—Paradox: Always mentioned on the Boulevard des Italiens between two puffs of a cigarette. [The Boulevard des Italiens was a haunt of opinion-formers]

PARENTS: Always disagreeable. Hide those that aren't rich.

PAUVRES—The poor: Concerning oneself with them takes the place of all other virtues.

PAYSAGES (DE PEINTRES)—Landscape: Always plates of spinach.

PEDANTISME—Pedantry: Should be scorned unless in reference to trifles.

PEDERASTIE—Pederasty: An illness which afflicts all men of a certain age.

PEIGNE POLONAISE—Polish plait: If you cut the hair it bleeds. [A common scalp disorder, thought to originate in the east]

PEINTURE SUR VERRE—Painting on glass: The secret of it is lost.

PENSER—To think: Difficult; things which force us to think are generally neglected.

PEROU—Peru: Country where everything is made from gold.

PEUR—Fear: Gives one wings.

PHAETON—Phaeton: Inventor of the carriage of the same name.

PHENIX—Phoenix: Nice name for a company of fire insurers.

PHILIPPE D'ORLEANS-EGALITE: Thunder against. Another cause of the Revolution. Committed all the crimes of this ill-fated epoch. [The Duc d'Orleans (1747-1793) was a revolutionary sympathiser, renounced his title and became 'Philippe-l'Egalité', and was later guillotined by his son]

PHILOSOPHIE—Philosophy: One must always snigger at it.

PIANO: Essential in a sitting room.

PIPE: Not acceptable apart from at seaside resorts.

PITIE—Pity: Always guard against it.

PLACE—Position: Always seek one.

POESIE—Poetry: Altogether useless: out of fashion.

POETE—Poet: Dignified synonym for simpleton (dreamer).

POLICE: Always wrong.

PONSARD: The only poet who had any sense.

POPILIUS: Inventor of a type of circle. [Caius Popilius Laenas who, in an obscure classical event of 170 BC, drew a circle around himself in the course of a discussion]

PORTEFEUILLE—Portfolio: Having one under the arm lends one the air of a minister.

PORTRAIT: The difficult thing is to get the smile right.

POURPRE—Crimson: A nobler word than red. Tell the story of the dog who discovered crimson while chewing a shellfish.

PRADON: Don't pardon him for having emulated Racine.

PRATIQUE—Practice: Superior to theory.

PRETRES—Priests: Sleep with their maids and have children which they call their nephews. Never mind, there are some good ones all the same.

PRIAPISME—Priapism: Cult of antiquity.

PRINCIPES—Principles: Always indisputable; one cannot tell their nature or quantity, no matter what, they are sacred.

PRISE DE TABAC—Pinch of snuff: Suits a professional gentleman.

PROGRES—Progress: Always ill-advised and too hasty.

PROSE: Easier to write than verse.

PUDEUR—Modesty: The most beautiful adornment of a woman.

PUCELLE—Maiden: Can only be used for Joan of Arc and with 'Orleans'.

PUNCH: Suits a lads' party. Source of mad delight. Extinguish the lights when setting it on fire. It produces wonderful flames!

PYRAMIDE—Pyramid: Useless work.

Q

QUADRATURE DU CERCLE—Squaring the circle: One

doesn't know what this is but one must shrug one's shoulders when it is mentioned.

R

RACINE: Randy devil!

RADEAU—Raft: Always of the 'Medusa' [A shipwreck with sensational accounts of cannibalism, painted by Géricault in 1819]

RADICALISME—Radicalism: All the more dangerous when it is latent.

RATE—Spleen: In the past runners had it removed.

RECONNAISSANCE—Gratitude: No need to express it.

RELIGION (LA): Part of the foundations of society. Is necessary for the masses, but not too much of it. 'The religion of our fathers' should be said with unction.

REPUBLICAINS—Republicans: Republicans are not all thieves, but thieves are all Republicans.

RICHESSE—Wealth: Takes the place of everything, even respect.

RIME—Rhyme: Never in accordance with reason.

RINCE-BOUCHE—Mouthwash: Sign of wealth in a house.

ROBE: Inspires respect.

ROMANS—Novels: Corrupt the masses. Less immoral in instalments than in a single volume. Only historical novels can be tolerated because they teach history. There are some novels written with the point of a scalpel, and others which rest on the point of a needle.

ROMANCES—Ballads: The men who sing them are pleasing to ladies.

RONSARD: Ridiculous with his Greek and Latin words.

ROUSSEAU: Believe that J.J. Rousseau and J.B. Rousseau

were brothers like the two Corneilles.

RUINES—Ruins: Make one dream and put poetry into a landscape.

S

SALON (FAIRE LE):   Literary debut which sets up a man very well.

SAPHIQUE ET ADONIQUE (VERS)—Poetry of Sappho and Adonis: Produces an excellent effect in an article of literary criticism.

SABOTS—Clogs: A rich man who had difficult beginnings always came to Paris in clogs.

SABRE: The French want to be governed by the sabre.

SAIGNER—To bleed: Let blood in the spring.

SAINT-BARTHELEMY—Saint Bartholomew: Old nonsense.
[The reference is to a massacre of Huguenots by Catholics, 24th August, 1572]

SAINTE-BEUVE: On Good Friday he ate nothing but cold meats. [Catholic day for having fish]

SAINTE-HELENE—Saint Helena: Island known for its rock.

SANTE—Health: Too much health causes illness.

SATRAPE—Satrap: A rich and debauched man.

SATURNALES—Saturnalia: Festivals of the Directory.

SAVANTS—Learned men: Make fun of them. To be learned one needs no more than a good memory and hard work.

SCUDERY: One must make fun of him without knowing whether he was a man or a woman. [Georges de Scudery (1601-1667) lent his name to his sister's romantic novels]

SERPENT—Snake: All poisonous.

SERVICE—Duty: To do one's duty to children means to clout them; to animals, to beat them; to servants, to chase them; to wrongdoers, to punish them.

SENEQUE—Seneca: Wrote on a gold desk.

SEVILLE: Famous for its barber.

SITE—Beauty spot: Place for writing poetry.

SOCIETE—Society: The enemies of society. That which brings about its downfall.

SOMNAMBULE—Somnambulist: Wanders around on rooftops at night.

SOUPES DE LA REGENCE—Regency suppers: Even more wit was dispensed than champagne.

SOUPIR—To sigh: One must exhale near a woman.

SPIRITUALISME—Spiritualism: The best system of philosophy.

STOICISME—Stoicism: Impossible.

SUFFRAGE UNIVERSEL—Universal suffrage: The last word in the political sciences.

SUICIDE: Proof of cowardice.

SYBARITES: Thunder against.

SYPHILIS: More or less everyone has it.

T

TABAC—Tobacco: Cause of all brain disease and diseases of the spinal cord.

TALLEYRAND: Express indignation.

TEMPS—Weather: Everlasting topic of conversation. Always grumble about it.

THEME—Prose composition: At school, prose composition proves hard work and unseen translation proves intelligence. But in the world one must laugh at eggheads who are good at prose composition.

TOILETTE DES DAMES—Ladies toilette: Troubles the imagination.

TOLERANCE (UN MAISON DE)—Whorehouse: Not one where there are tolerant opinions.

TOUR—Lathe: Essential to have one in your attic in the country for rainy days.

TRANSPIRATION DES PIEDS—Sweaty feet: Sign of good health.

U

UKASE: Call any authoritarian decree a ukase; this annoys the government.

UNIVERSITE—University: *Alma mater.*

V

VACCINE: Only consort with people who are vaccinated.

VALSE—Waltz: Express indignation against.

VEILLE—Gathering: Country ones are moral.

VELOURS—Velvet: On clothes is a sign of distinction and wealth.

VENTE—Sale: Buying and selling is the purpose of life.

VIELLARD—Old man: Whenever there is a flood or a storm etc, old men can never remember having seen an equivalent.

VINS—Wines: Topic of conversation among men. Bordeaux is the best since it is prescribed by doctors. The worse it is, the more natural.

VISIR—Vizier: Trembles at the sight of a piece of cord.

VOISINS—Neighbours: Try to get them to do you services

without it costing you anything.

VOLTAIRE: Famous for his dreadful 'rictus'. Superficial learning.

VOITURES—Carriages: More convenient to hire one than to own one: this way one has neither the bother of servants nor of horses which are always getting ill.

VOYAGE—Journey: Should be made at speed.

W

WAGNER: Snigger when one hears his name, and make jokes about the music of the future.

Y

YVETOT: See Yvetot and die (and Naples, and Seville).